CROSSROADS

3 paths to nature

GLASS, BLOOM, BERNDT

CROSSROADS
3 Paths to Nature

Landscape, Nature and Wildlife Photography

e-mail Markos Berndt at: markosphoto@markosphoto.com
Website: **http://markosphoto.com**

e-mail Minerva Bloom at: minerva_bloom@yahoo.com
Website: **www.zazzle.com/moonrisings**

e-mail Gary Glass at: digitaleyes@hotmail.com
Website: **www.garyglass.com**

Printed in the United States of America
ISBN: 978-0-557-92270-3

Published through
Lulu Enterprises, Inc.
3131 RDU Center, Suite 210
Morrisville, NC 27560
www.lulu.com

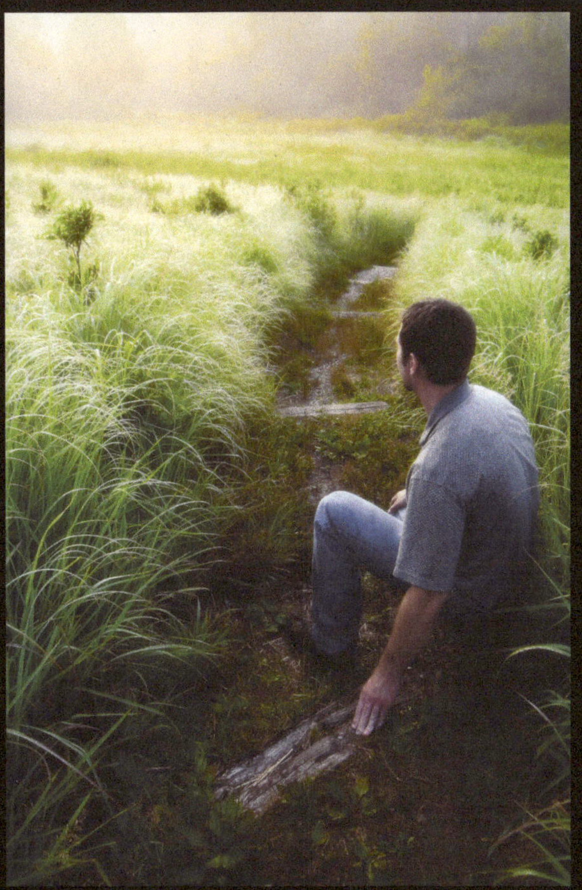

"Reaching a crossroad often means leaving your past behind, and looking into the mirror hoping the path you take is the right one. Especially when the path back is uphill."

Gary Glass

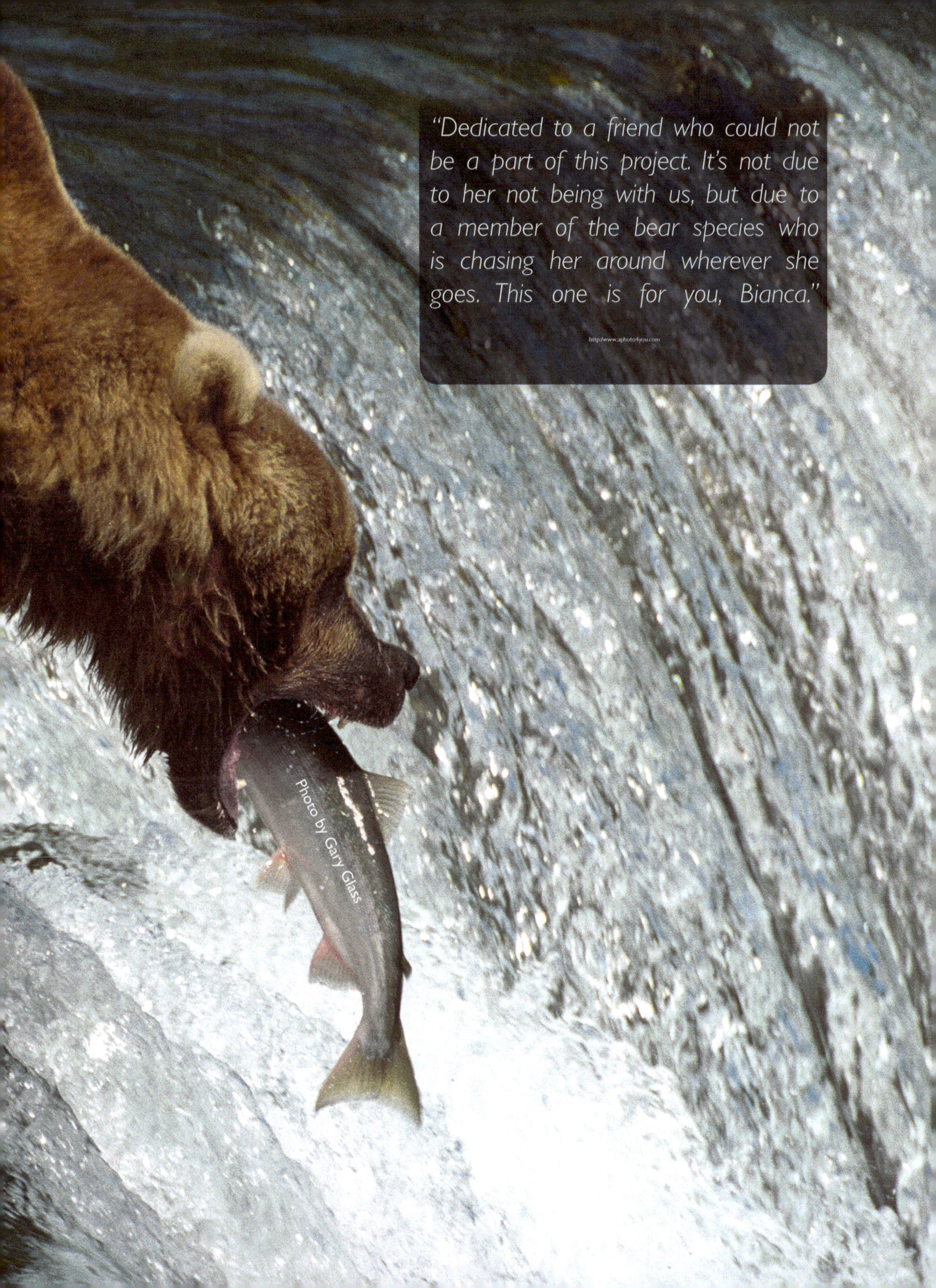

"Dedicated to a friend who could not be a part of this project. It's not due to her not being with us, but due to a member of the bear species who is chasing her around wherever she goes. This one is for you, Bianca."

Photo by Gary Glass

TABLE OF CONTENTS

INTRO

Crossroads, an intersection of roads also used metaphorically as a place where other things – both physical and abstract – meet. And that is where we begin with this book: it brings 3 individuals together. Not that they are at a crossroad, but the fact that their love for photography brought them together to this point.

The three of us first crossed roads at a mutual art site a few years ago, and it didn't take long to find our common interest in photography. Soon friendships developed. Markos realized we shared the same love for the American Southwest and proposed creating this book, to explore the convergence of three photographers from three different corners of the United States (Minerva-Florida, Gary-California and Markos-Wisconsin), each with our own particular approach and vision. While this book began showcasing the Southwest, it also expanded into our individual passion as photographers.

Markos is fascinated by water, and his images of Wisconsin and the Smoky Mountains portray his love of moving water, as well as in its frozen state. Minerva is fond of travel photography and while not all her journeys are featured in this book, one can see the eye she has for capturing images to pique the interest of tourists and viewers alike, to traveling destinations. While my own tastes run the gamut of wildlife, landscape as well as general photography. I do however have a special fondness for photographing the areas of Yellowstone and Grand Tetons.

I would like to thank Markos for inviting me to participate in this venture he conceived, as well as it being a pleasure to work with Minerva once again.

-Gary Glass

Gary Glass

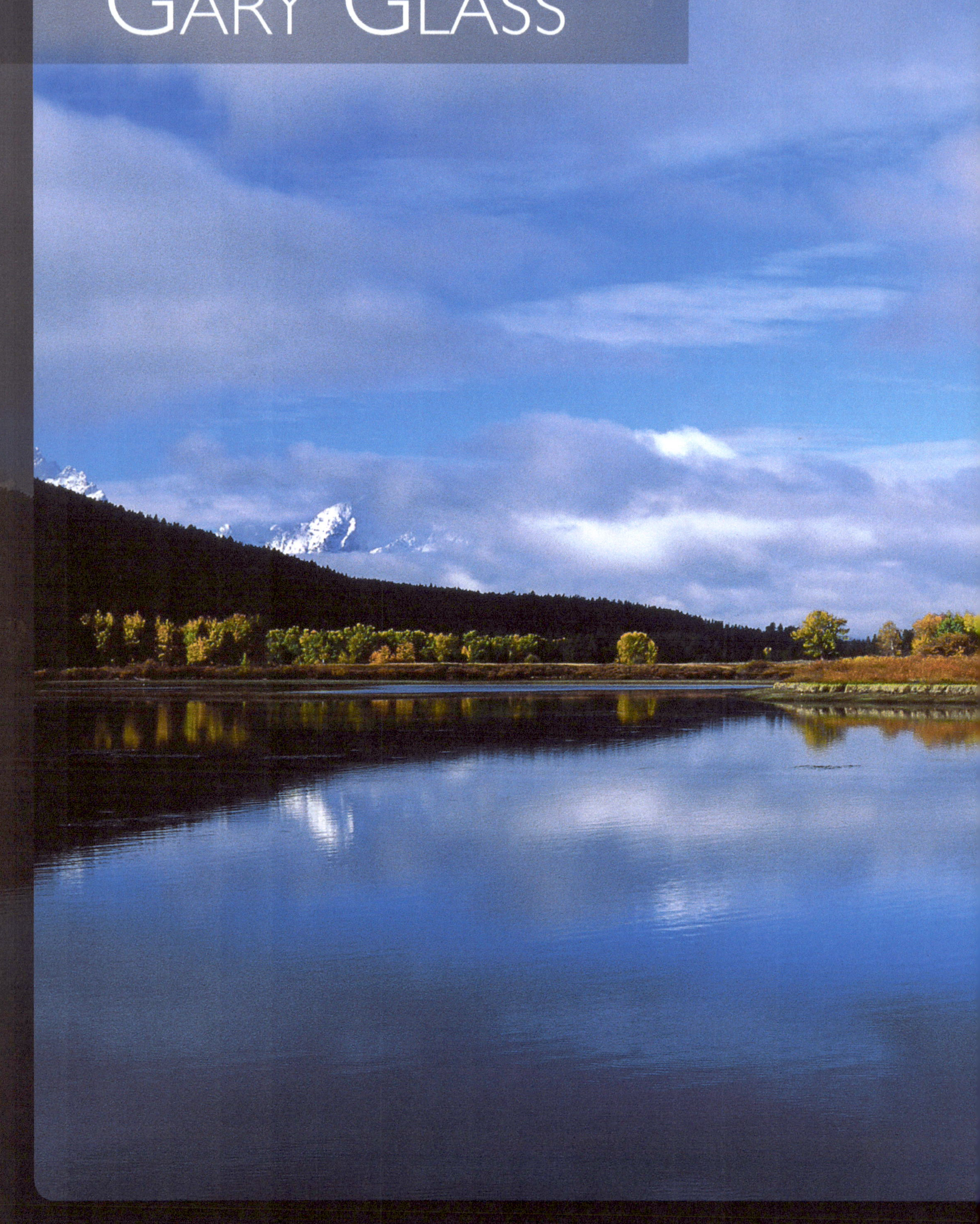

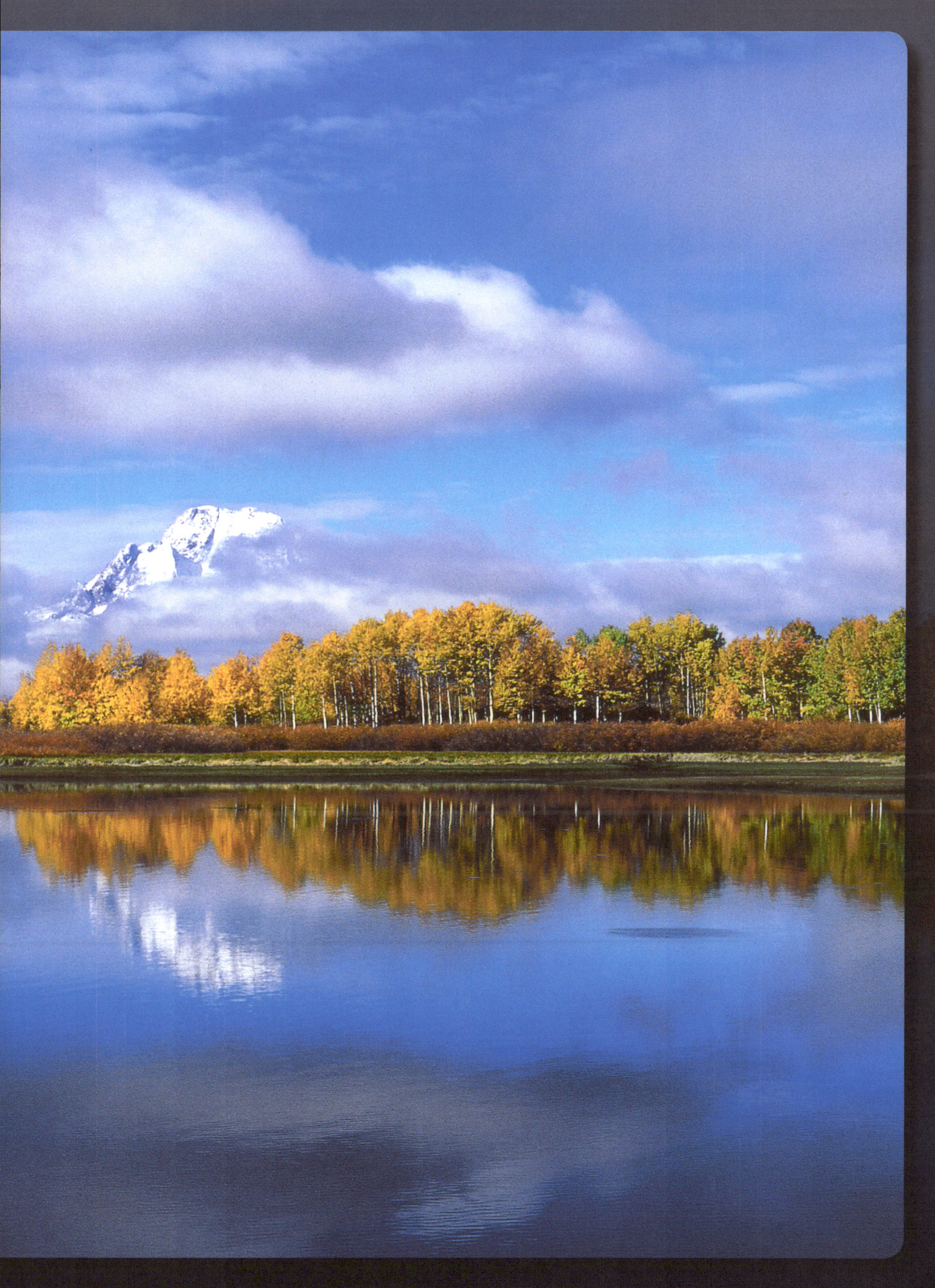

Photography has always been a part of my life since I was about 11 years old. I would sneak out with my mother's camera to photograph the friends and wildlife that I would come across on my daily sojourns. I was always bringing something from the wild to my home, much to the chagrin of my Mom. My love for the outdoors was nurtured by my Dad's love of camping and road trips. He would take us off to the Sequoias/Yosemite National Parks, Arizona, Yellowstone/Tetons and on trips up and down the California Coast, as well as trips to his native home in Kentucky.

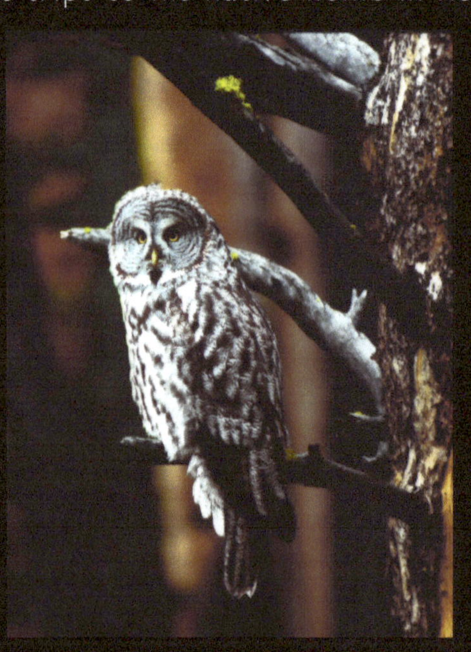

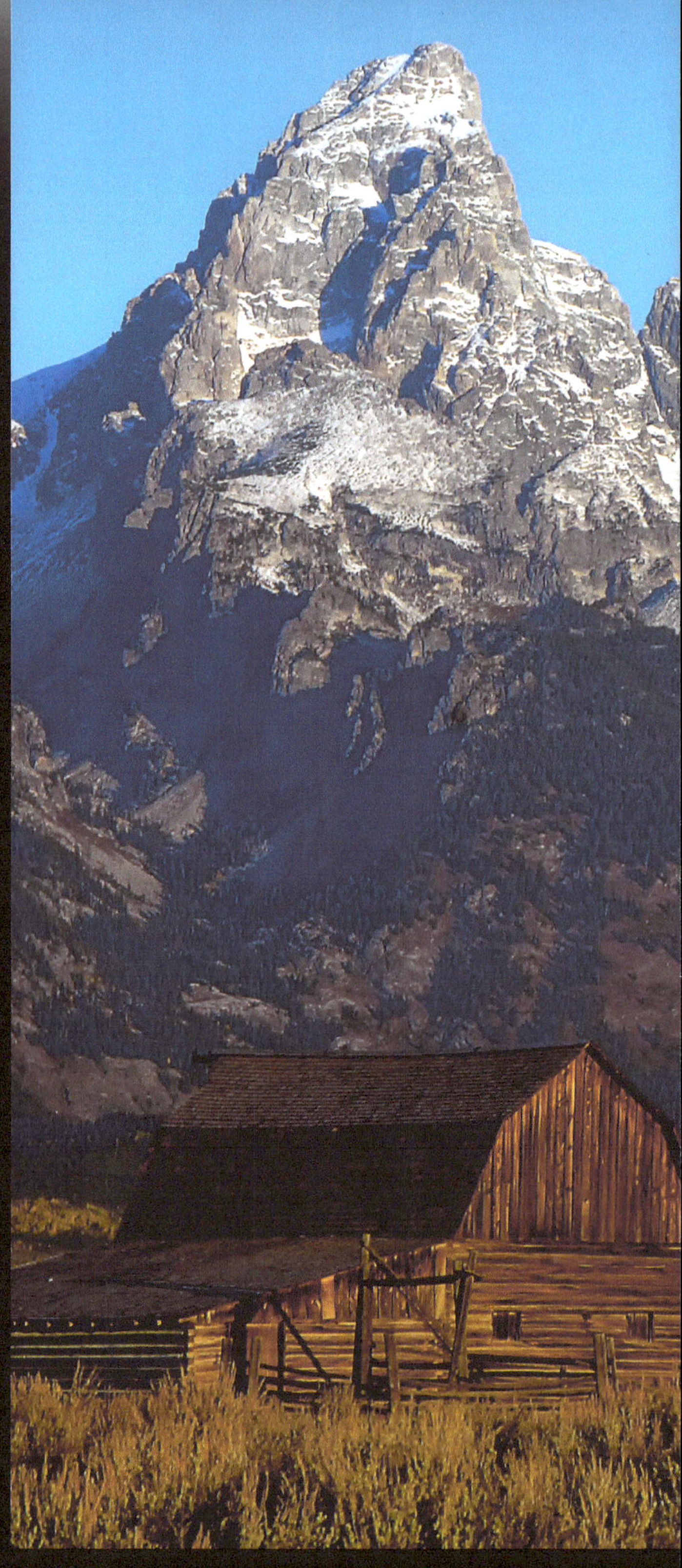

So one can see, I was born to roam. Roam I did, through the San Francisco Presidio where I grew up to the areas of Southern California where we relocated to. Most of my free time was used to go on camping trips, vacations or any activities that took me outdoors. On those excursions, I would come across breathtaking visions of scenery and wildlife and wanting to share those with others, I found that trying to articulate into words, just did not reflect the wonders I had witnessed. So once again, I turned to my friend the camera and started documenting the sights I was witnessing.

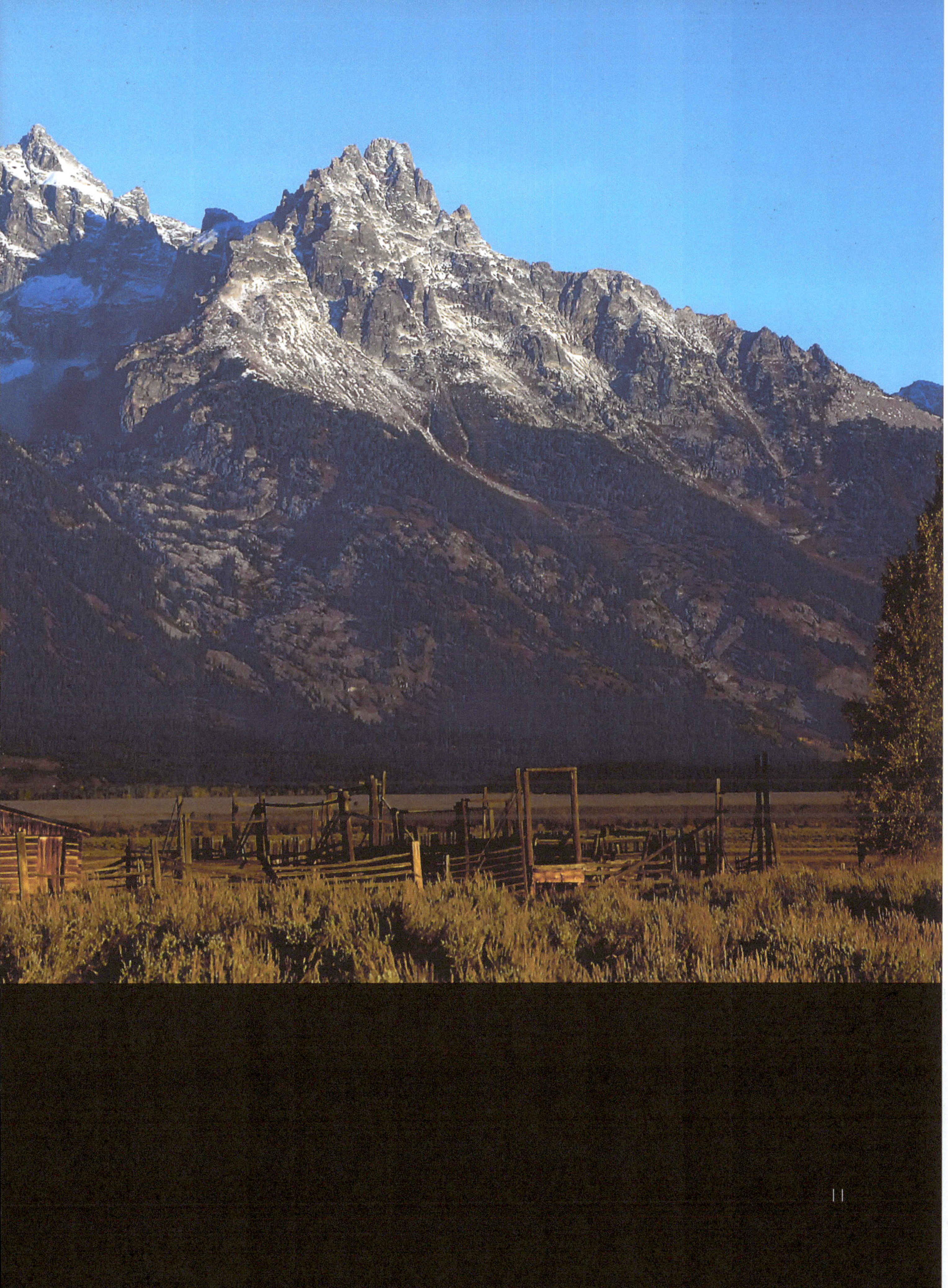

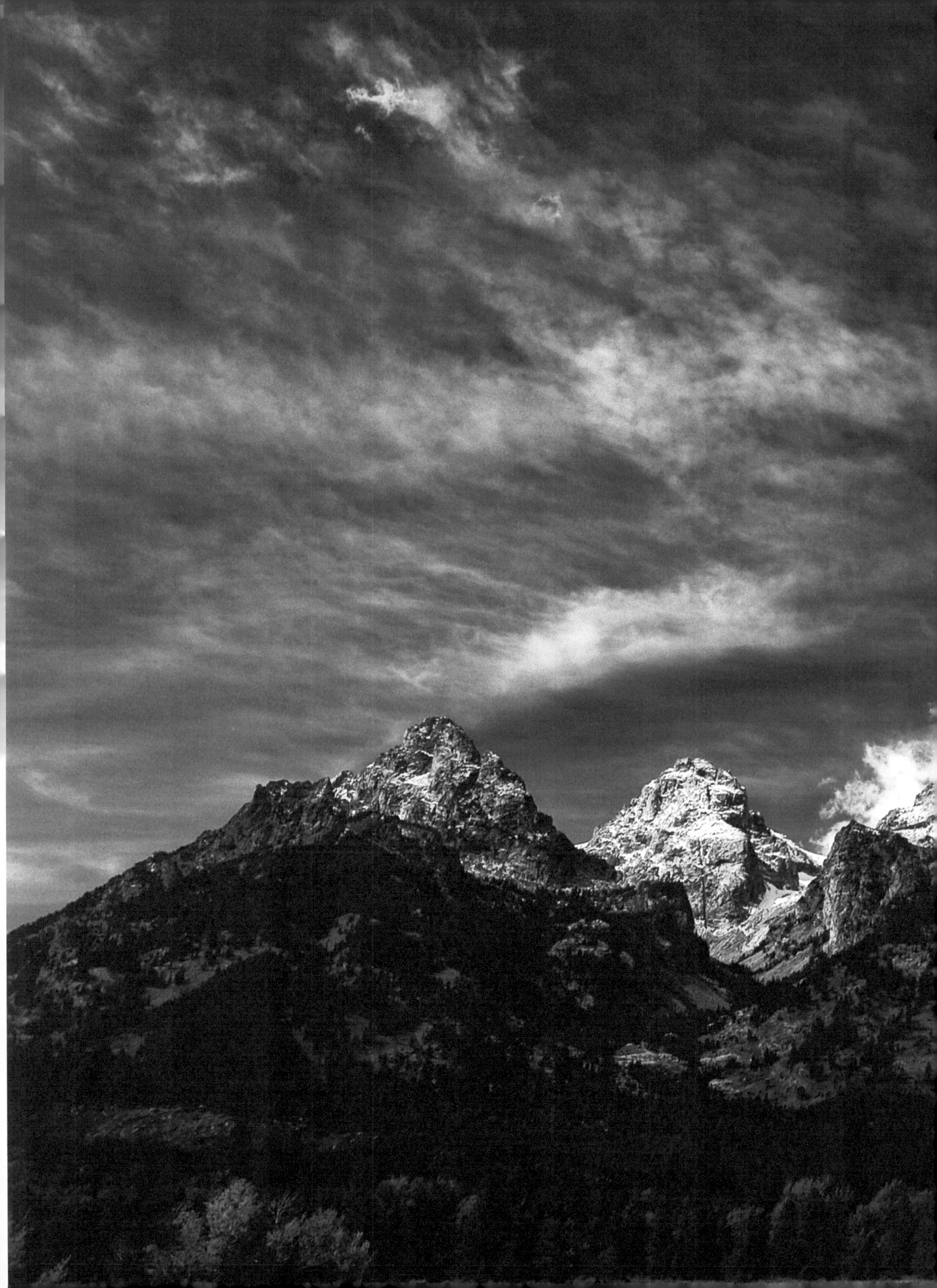

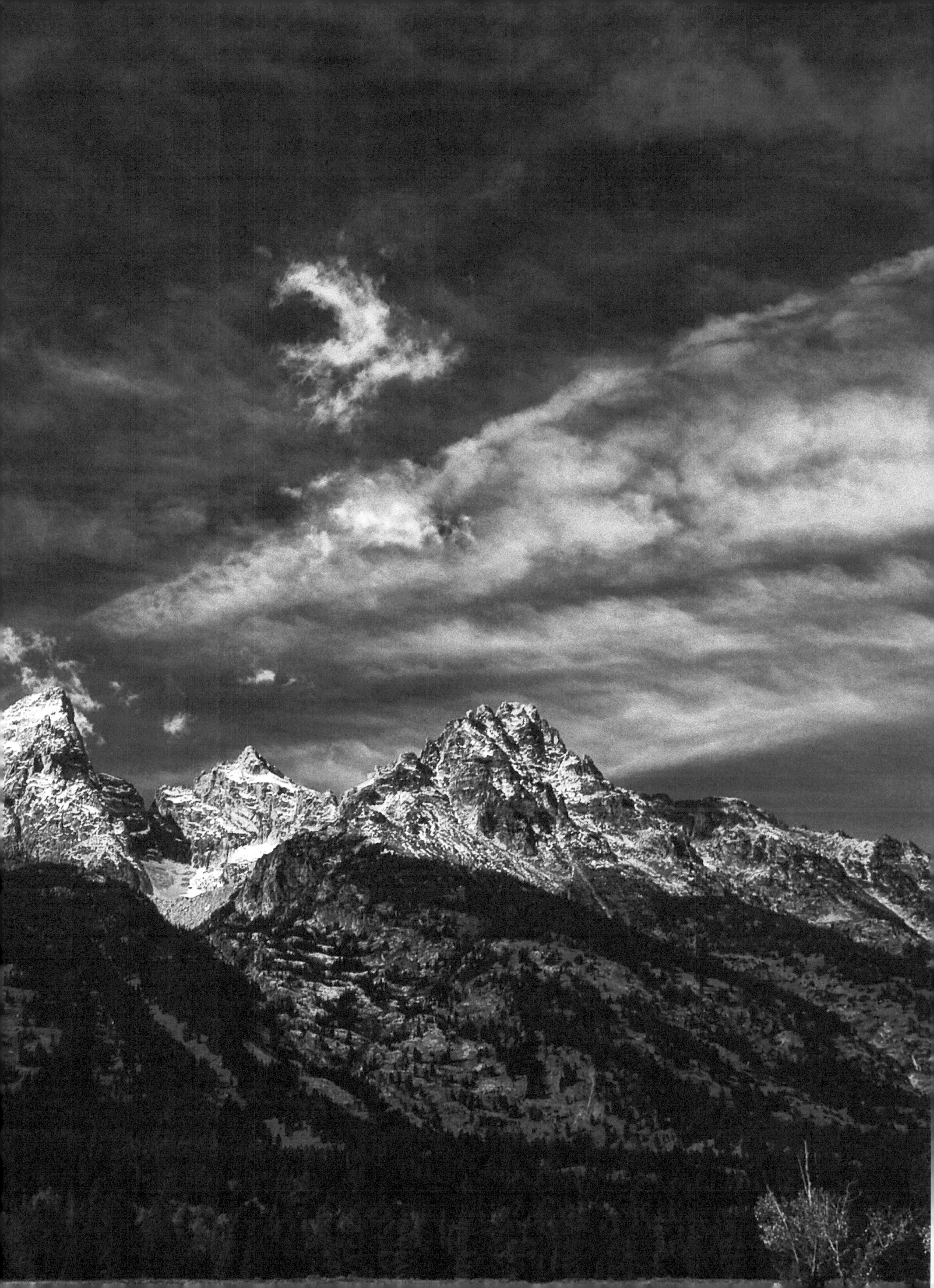

My early photographic trips/camping were to Yosemite and the California and Oregon coasts. Later, I started revisiting areas my Dad had taken us: Arizona/Sedona, Kentucky as well as revisiting a long lost friend, Yellowstone/Tetons. For me there is just something visceral about Yellowstone and the Tetons that I cannot really put into words.

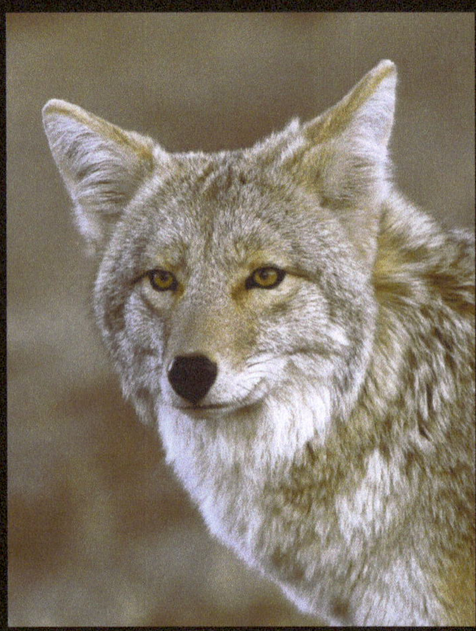

I just know that every time I visit, I feel such a kindred spirit and a sense of belonging that I find myself going back year after year. It has become a second home for me as well as having a special place in my heart.

Another place I first photographed 10 years ago is Alaska. I am just in awe of the expanse of the Alaskan mountain range, the sheer majesty of Mount Denali/McKinley and Denali Park, the animals that roam across the tundra and its colors in fall. It offers a lot for a photographer willing to spend some time there to capture its beauty and splendor.

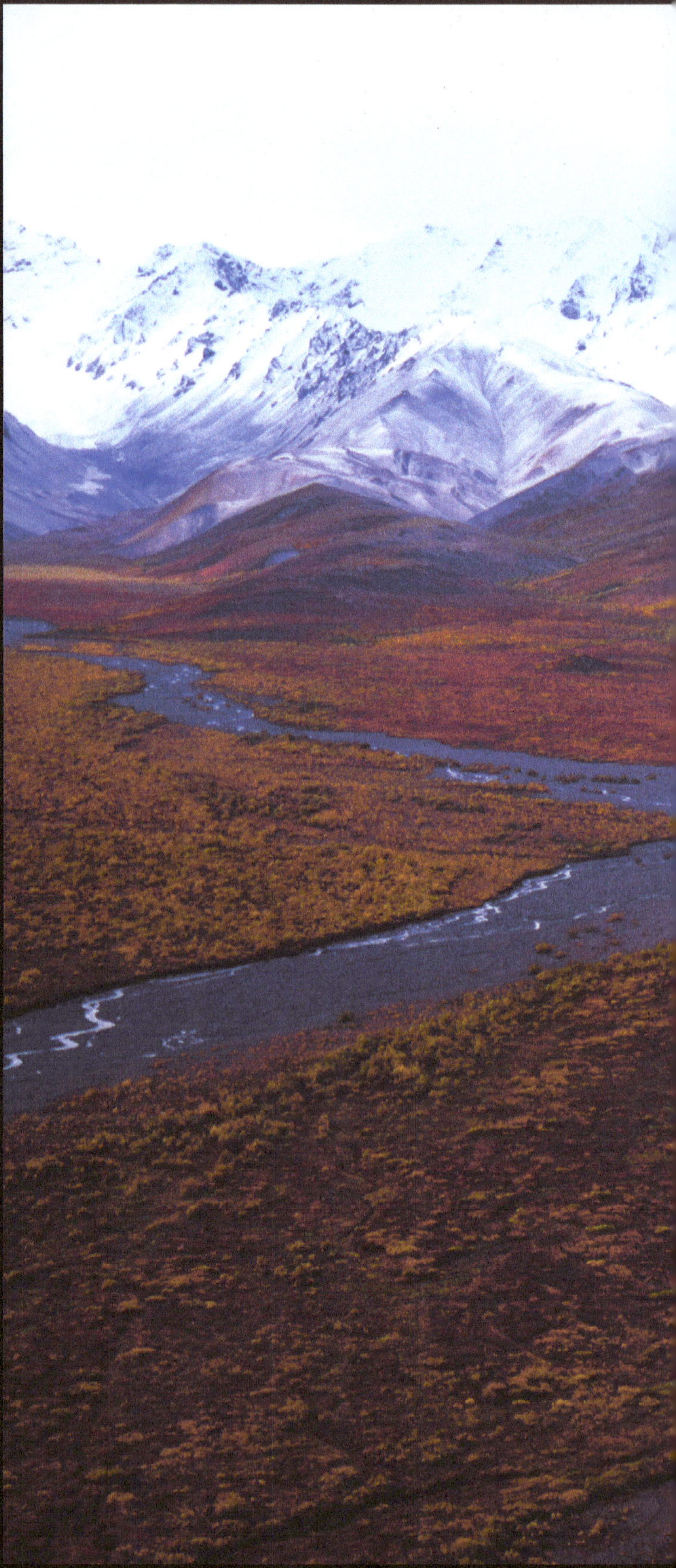

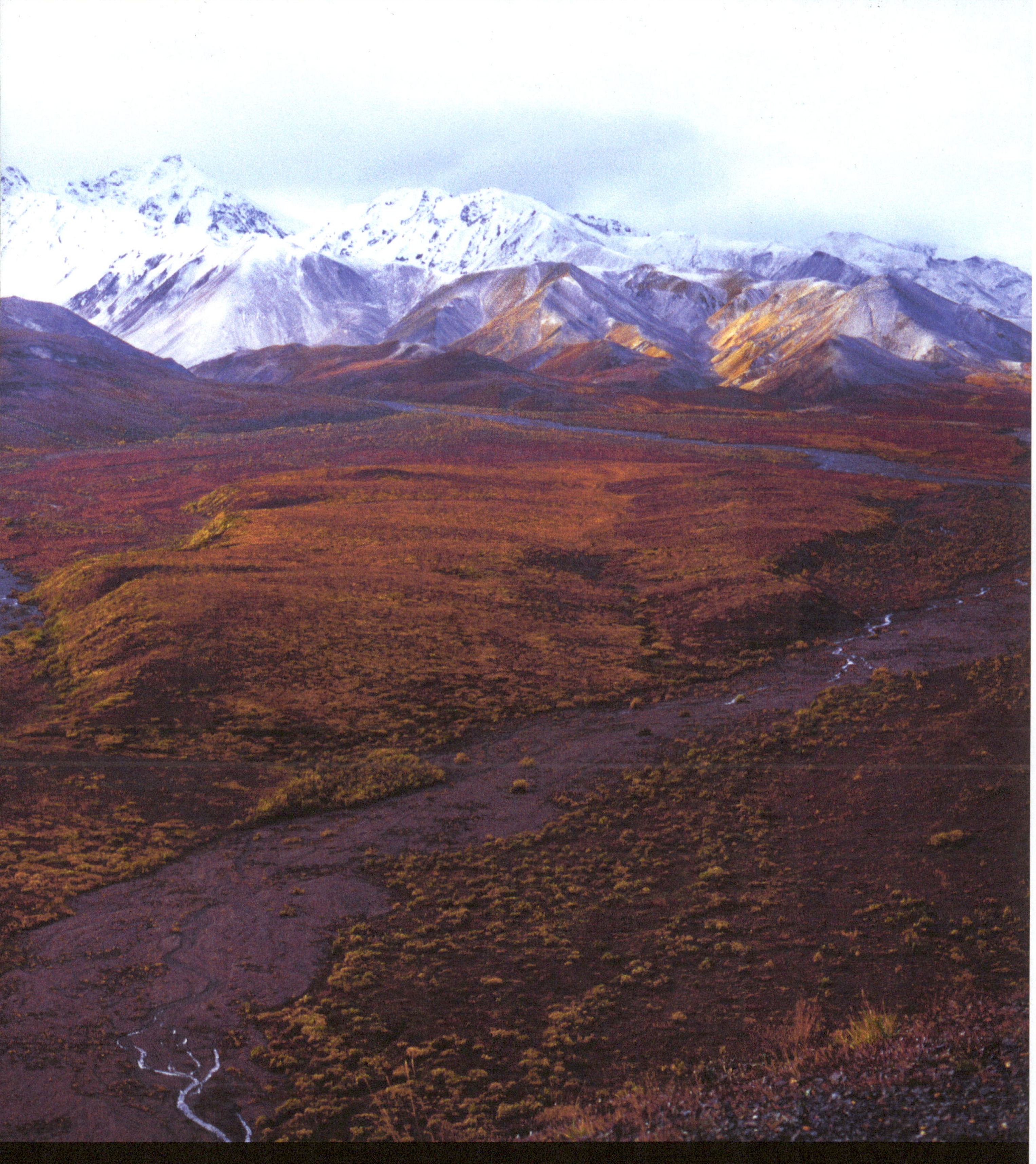

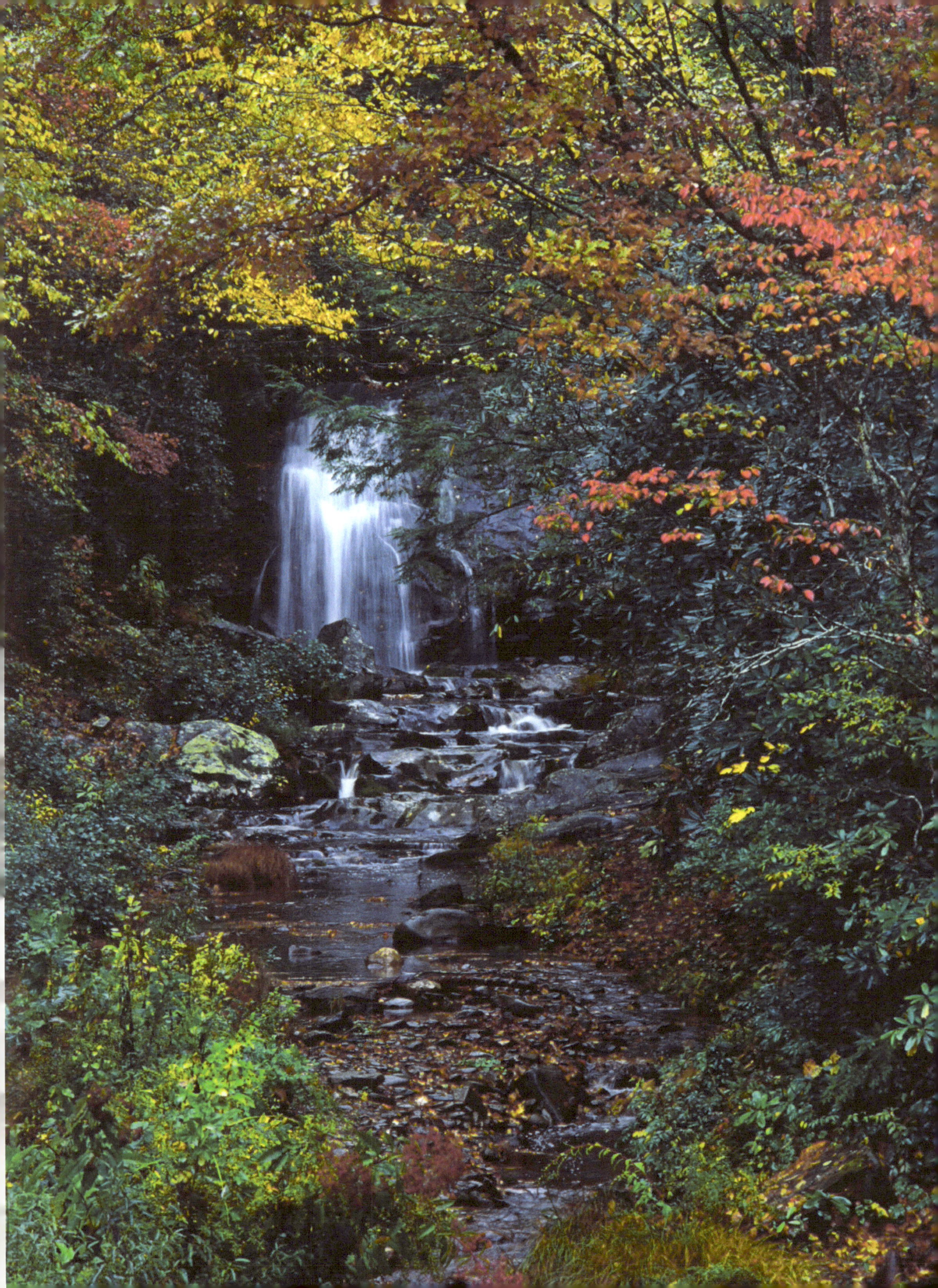

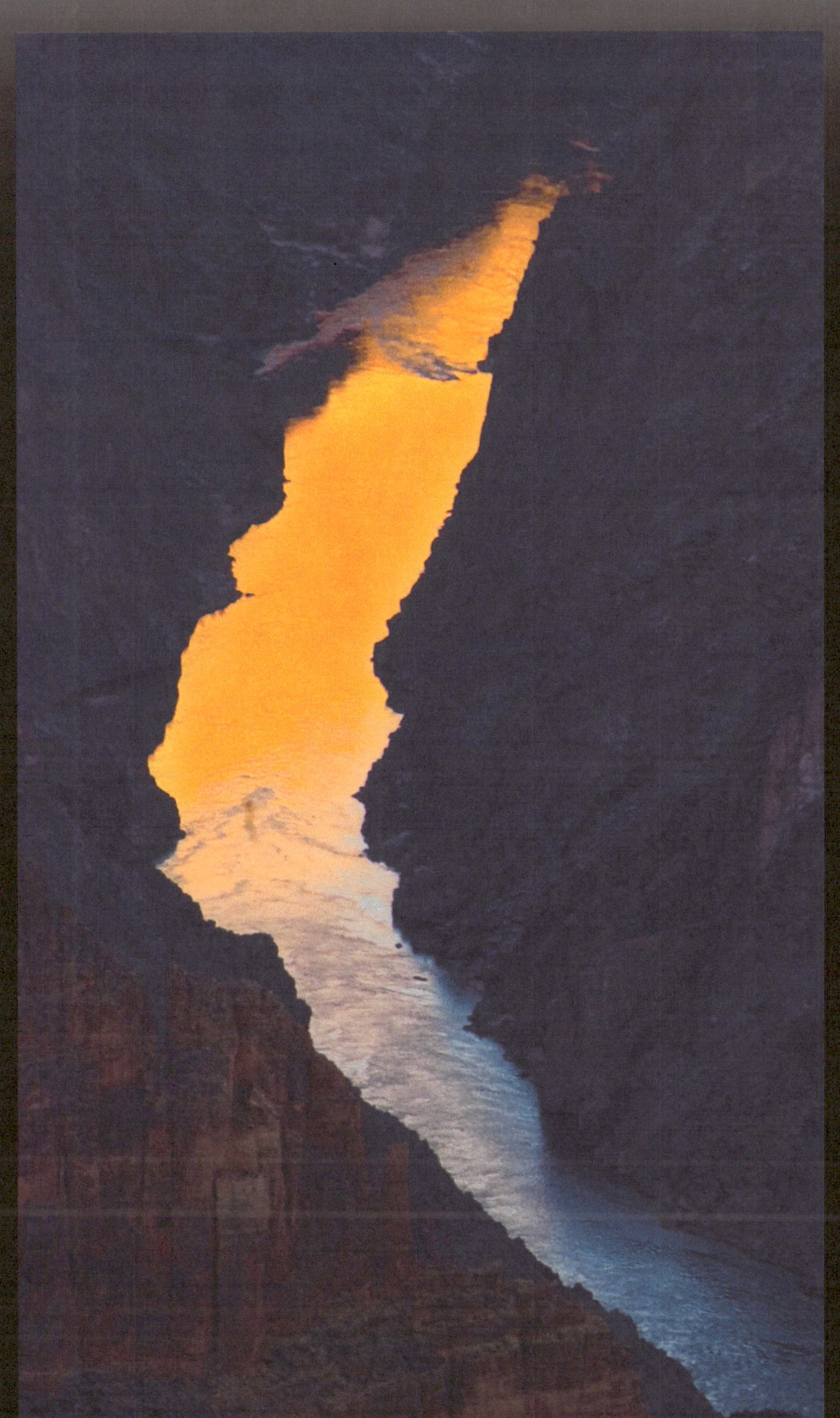

A view of the Colorado River from Hopi Point, coursing its way through the Grand Canyon as the sun begins to set.

"As the sun sets, the diverse light that illuminates throughout the canyon and it's walls, creates a palette of hues which are always shifting and changing, turning shadows into Gold. This sublime sleight of hand-magic shows Nature to be the true Alchemist."
-Gary Glass

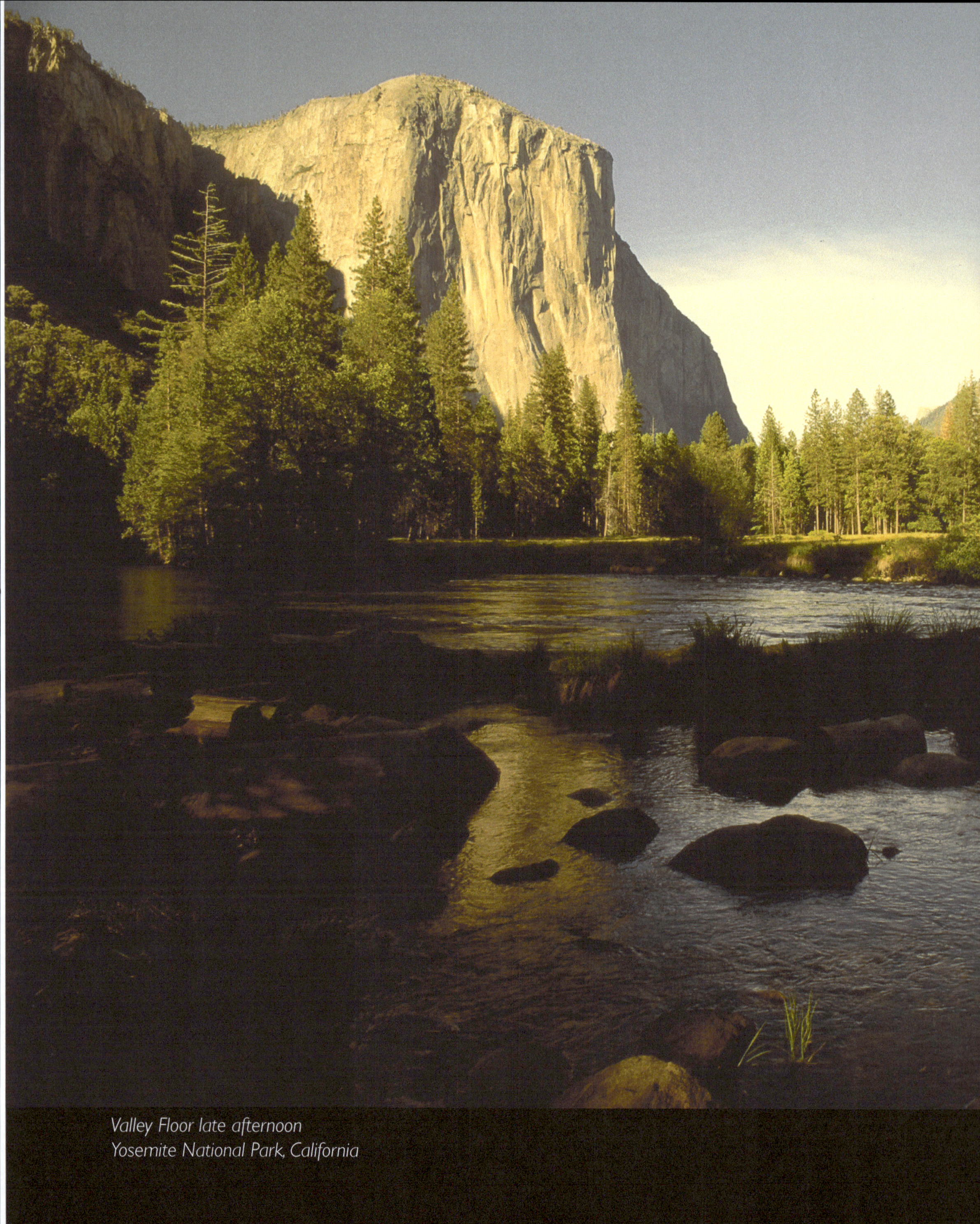

Valley Floor late afternoon
Yosemite National Park, California

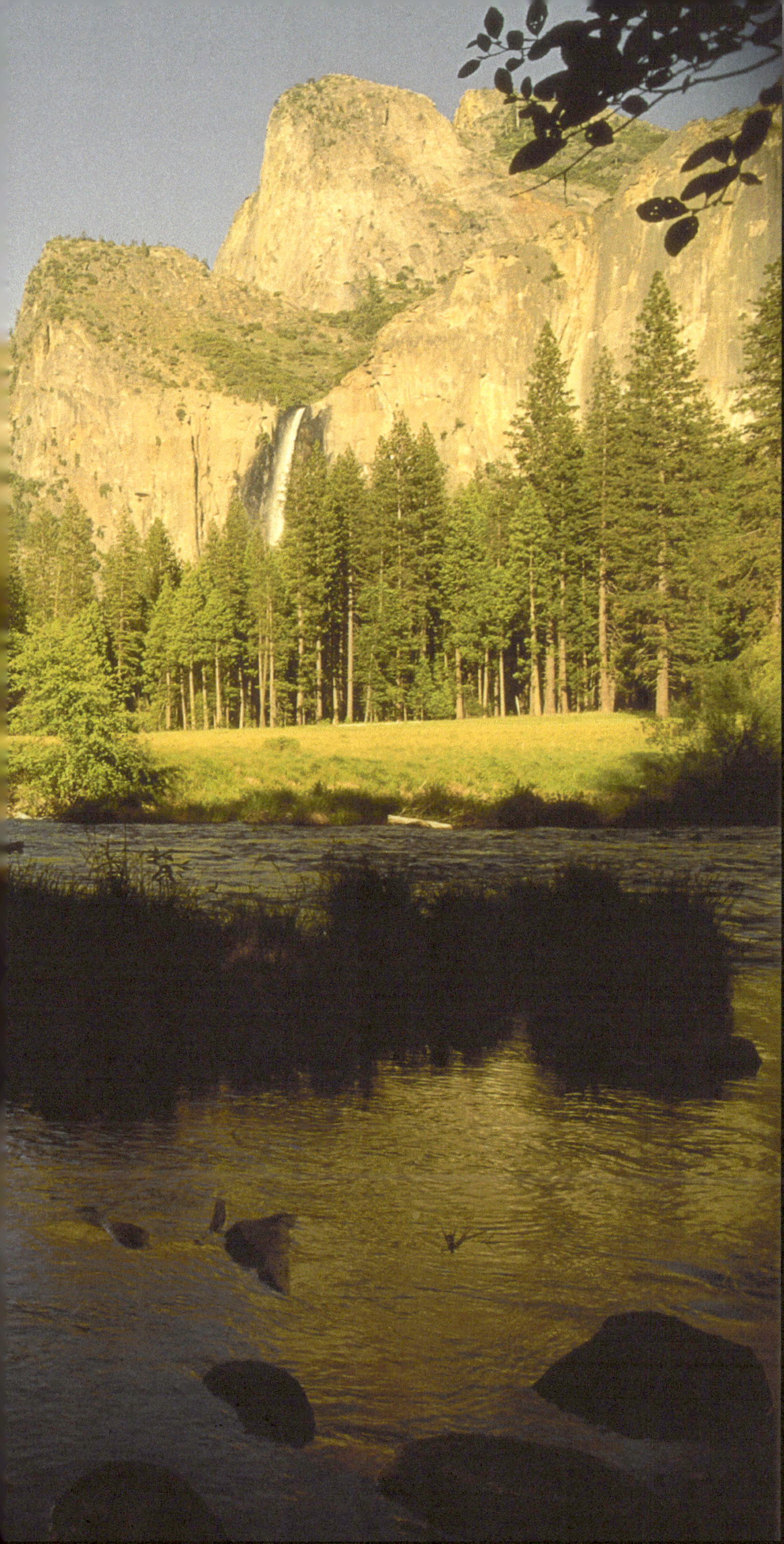

While I am out photographing, I first and foremost try to capture the awe or beauty that stirs an emotion within me as I reflect upon the landscape for my own satisfaction and pleasure. My hopes are that if I do my job correctly, the images will stir emotion in the viewer's heart and soul as well. Having experienced some of the grandeur we are surrounded with in nature, I envision that in some small way if I can carry the torch along with others to help preserve that which we have, in the grand tradition of those that came before us, for they had the foresight and wisdom to protect and preserve what they saw as Nature's Precious treasures. Hopefully that same sentiment will be passed along for future generations to partake and enjoy as we did.

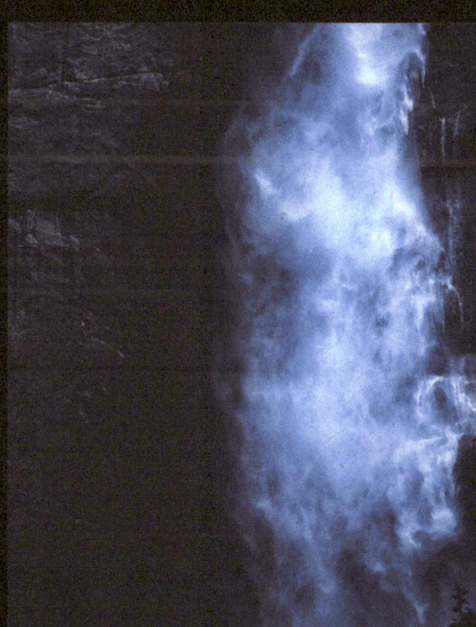

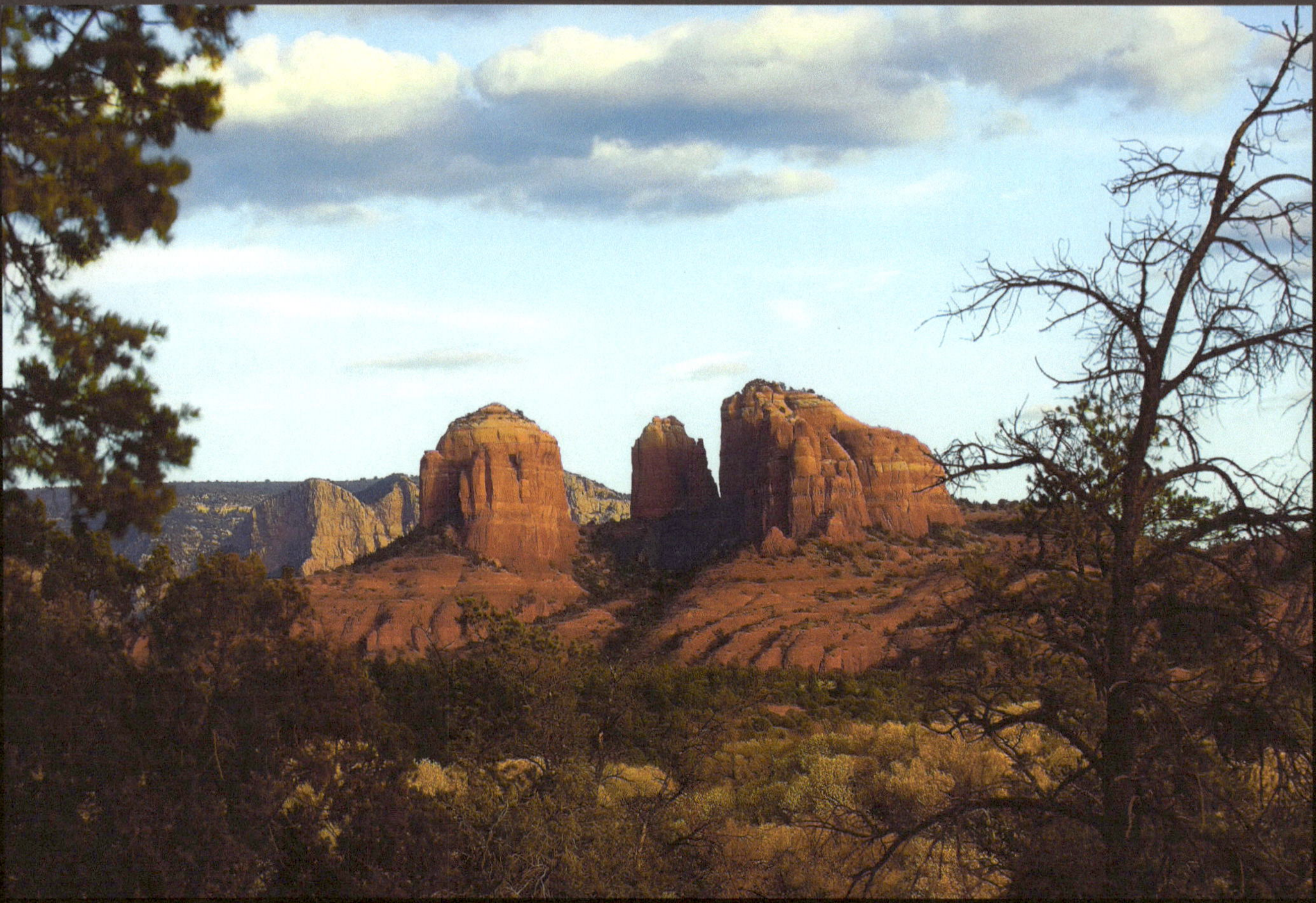

Cathedral Rock as viewed from Red Rock Loop Road, Sedona, Arizona

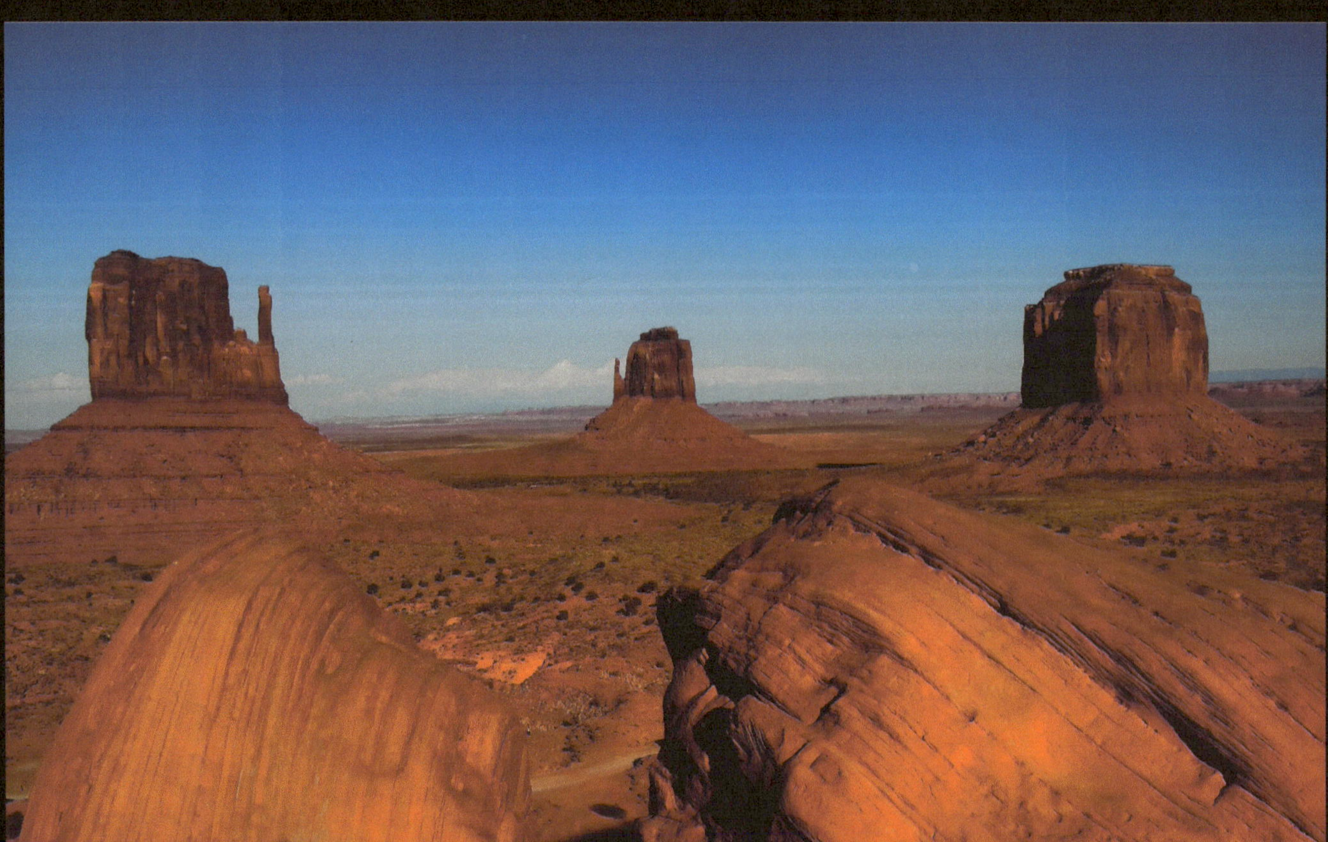

View of the Mittens and Merrick Butte, Monument Valley, Utah/Arizona

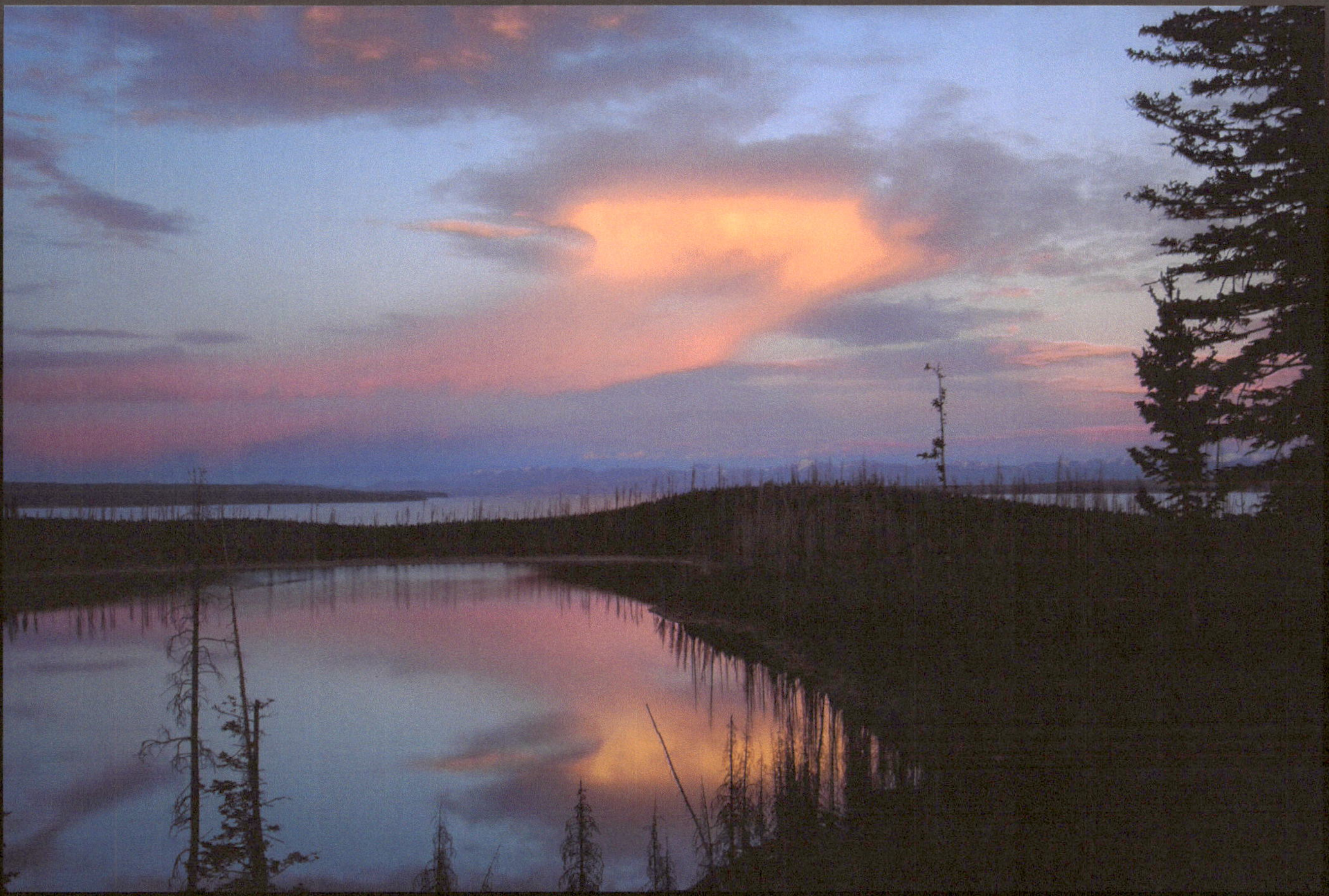

Sunset over Duck Lake, West Thumb Geyser Basin area of Yellowstone, Wyoming

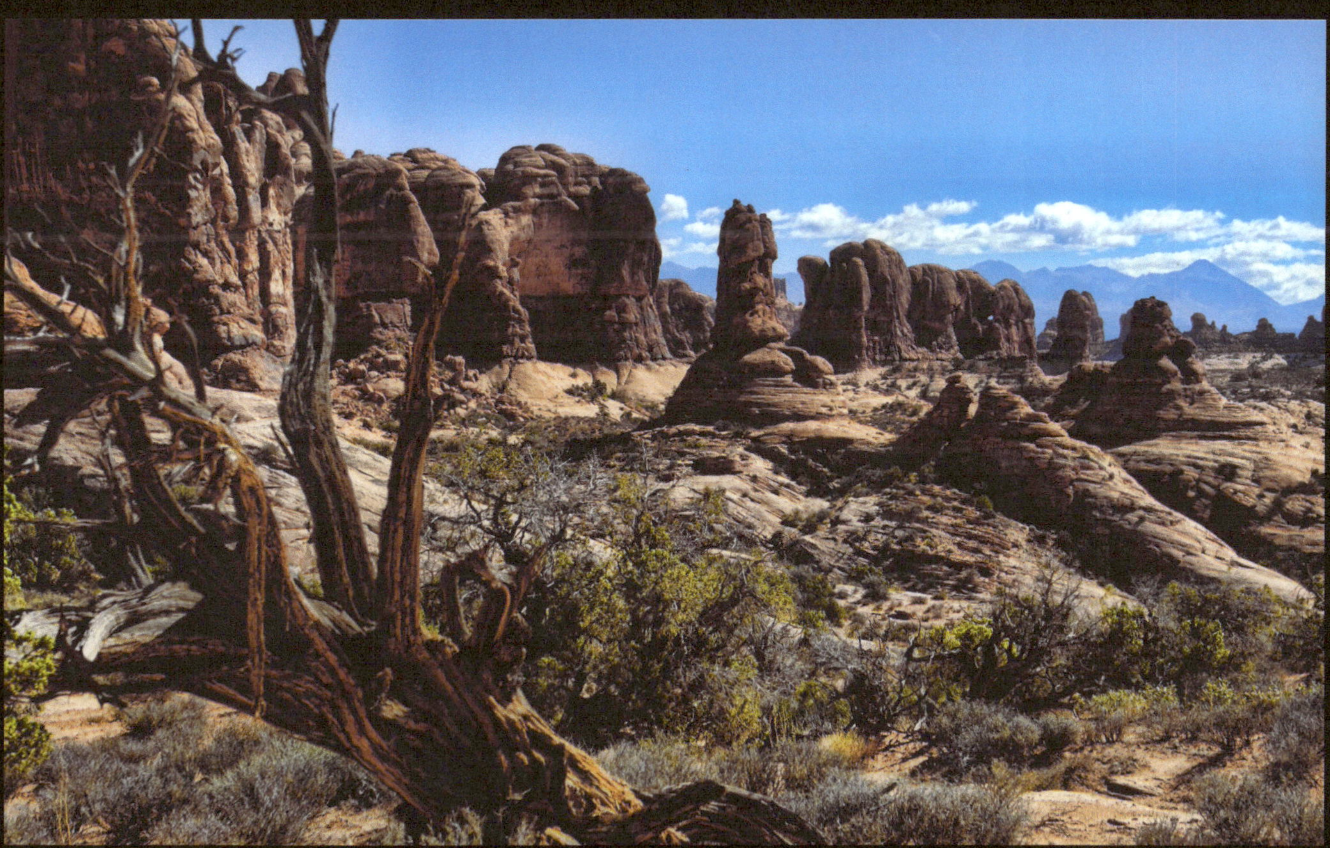

Garden of Eden View, Arches National Park, Utah

Within my journey down the path of nature I'll continue to learn ever more than I knew before, in a quest to stir the emotions.

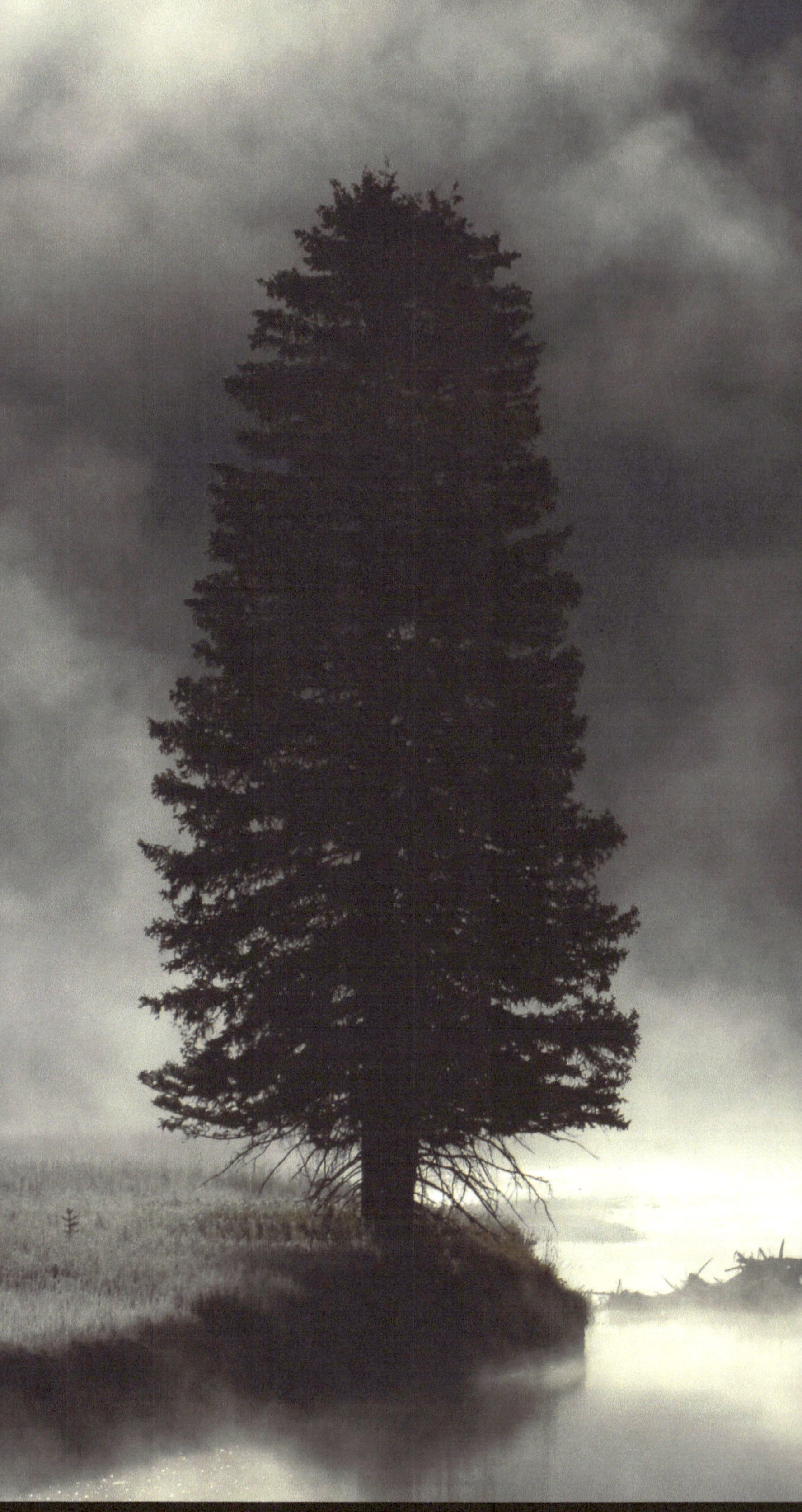

Morning Mist on the Snake River
Yellowstone National Park, Wyoming.

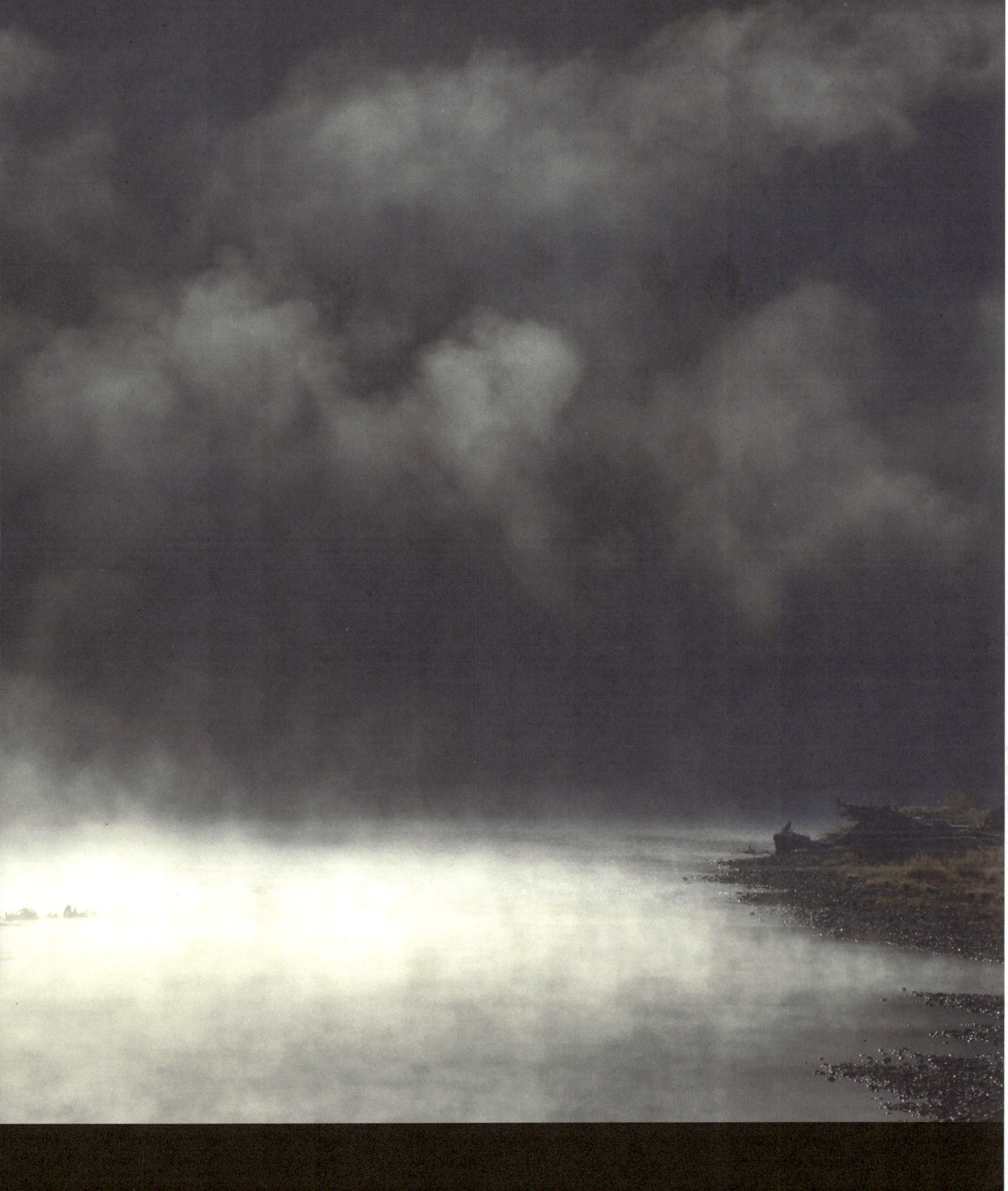

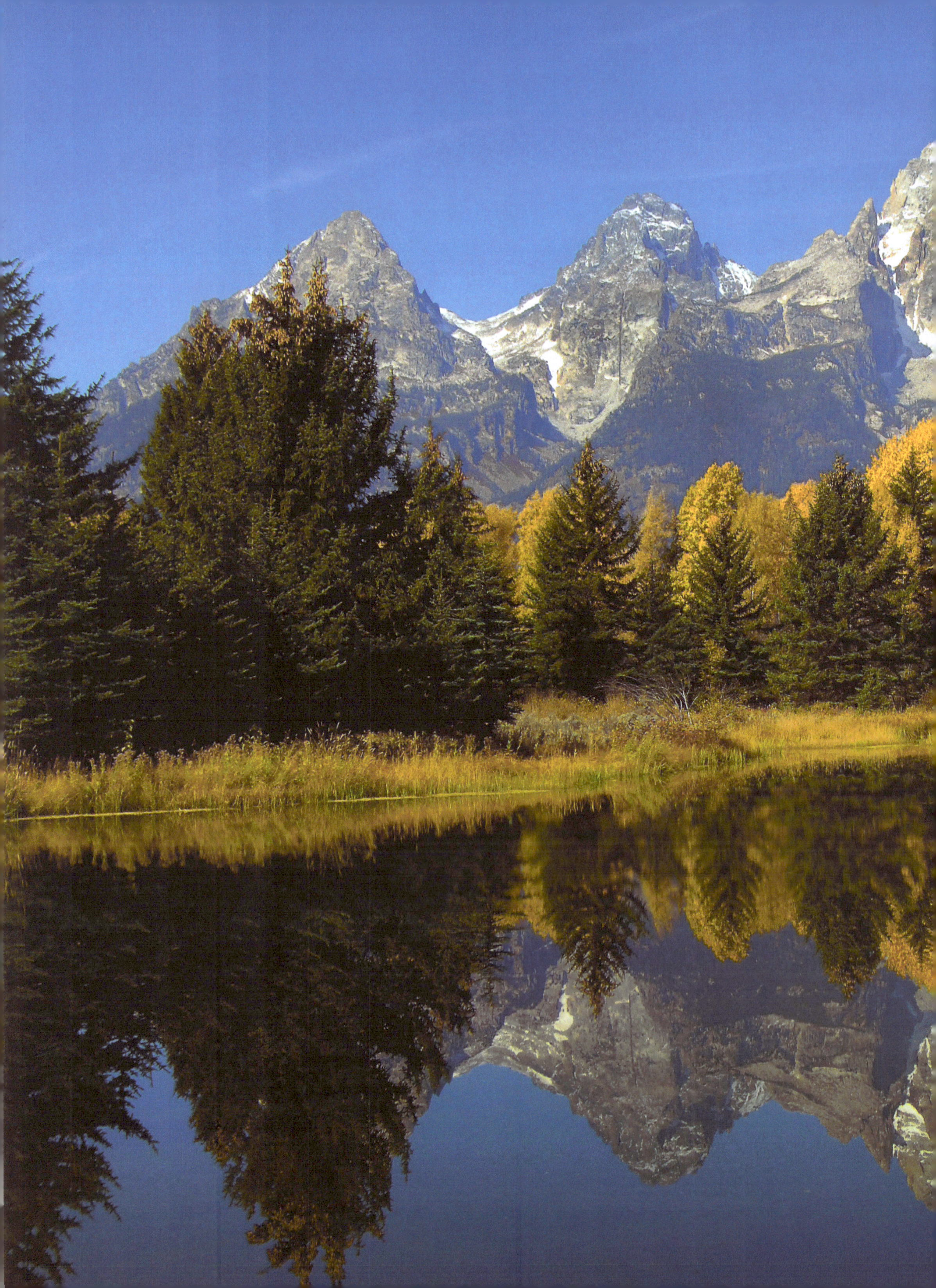

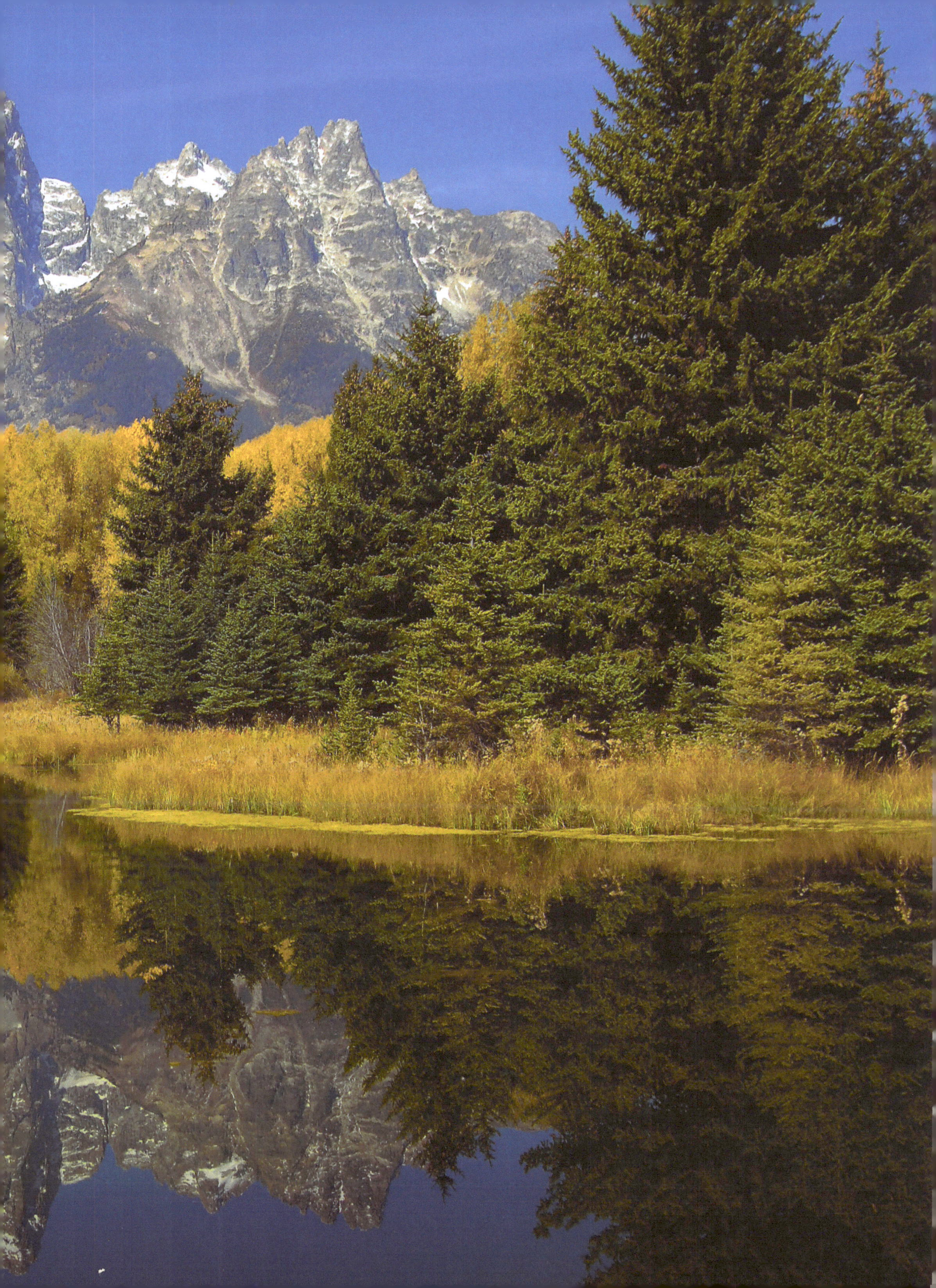

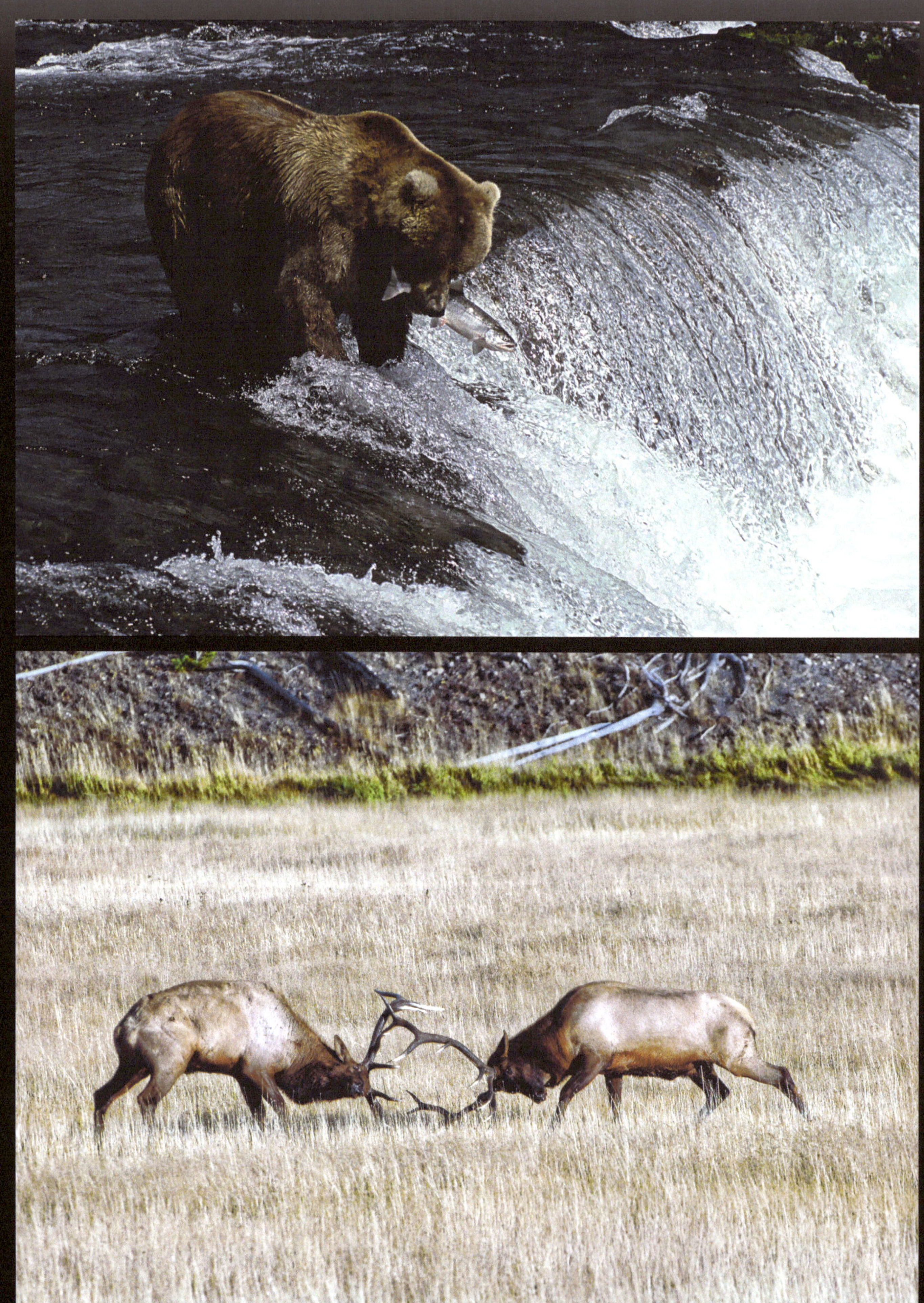

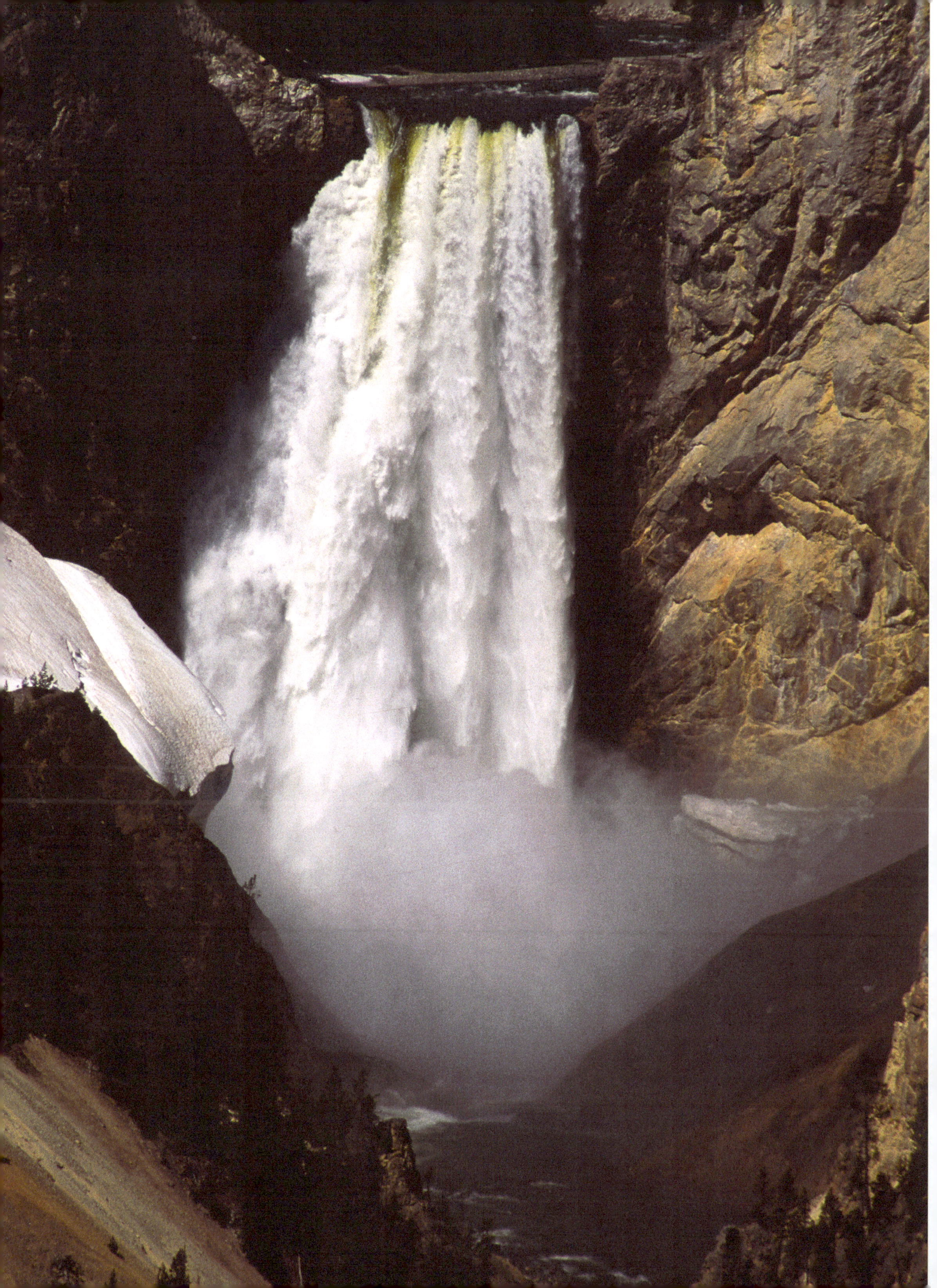

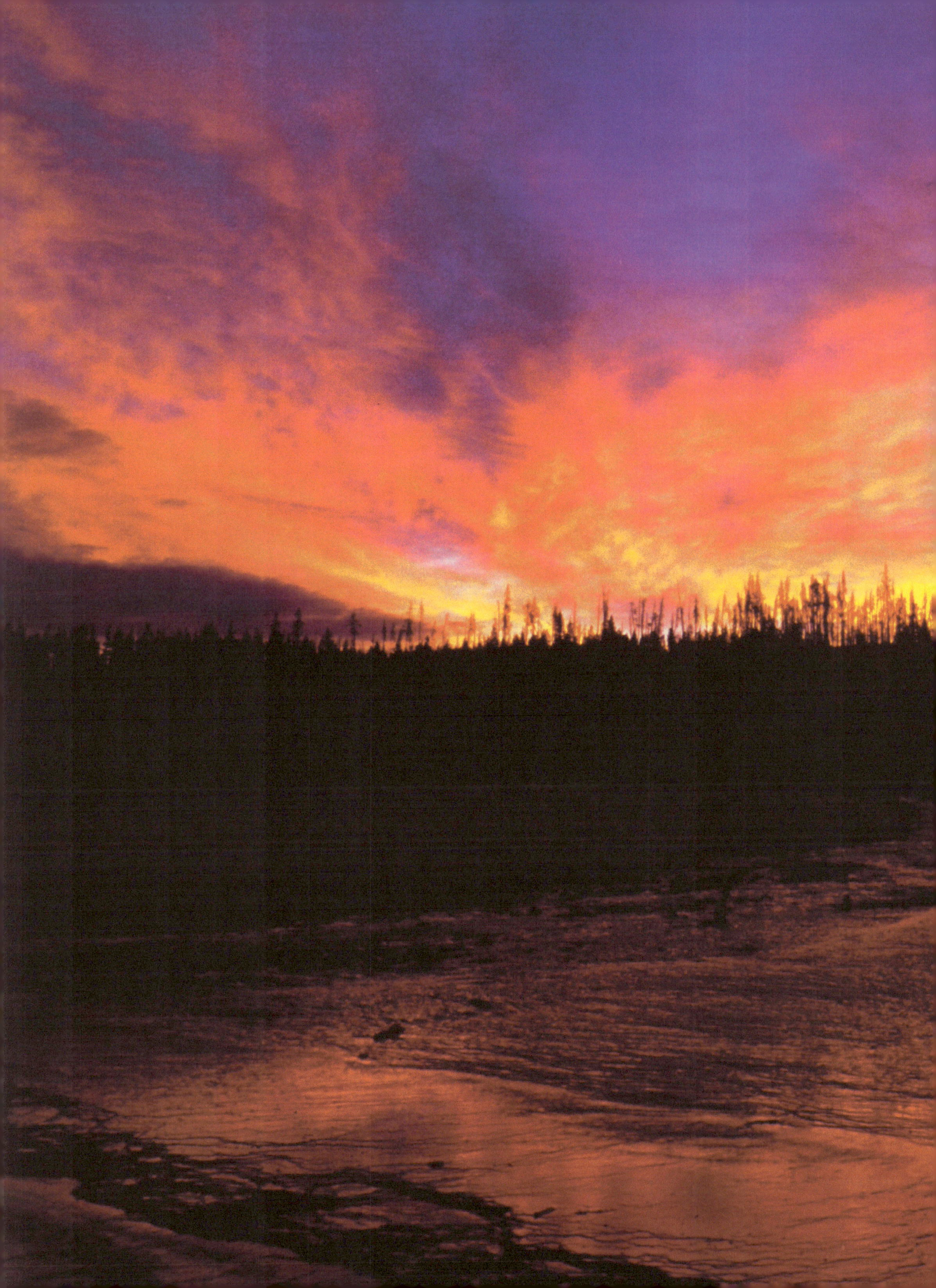

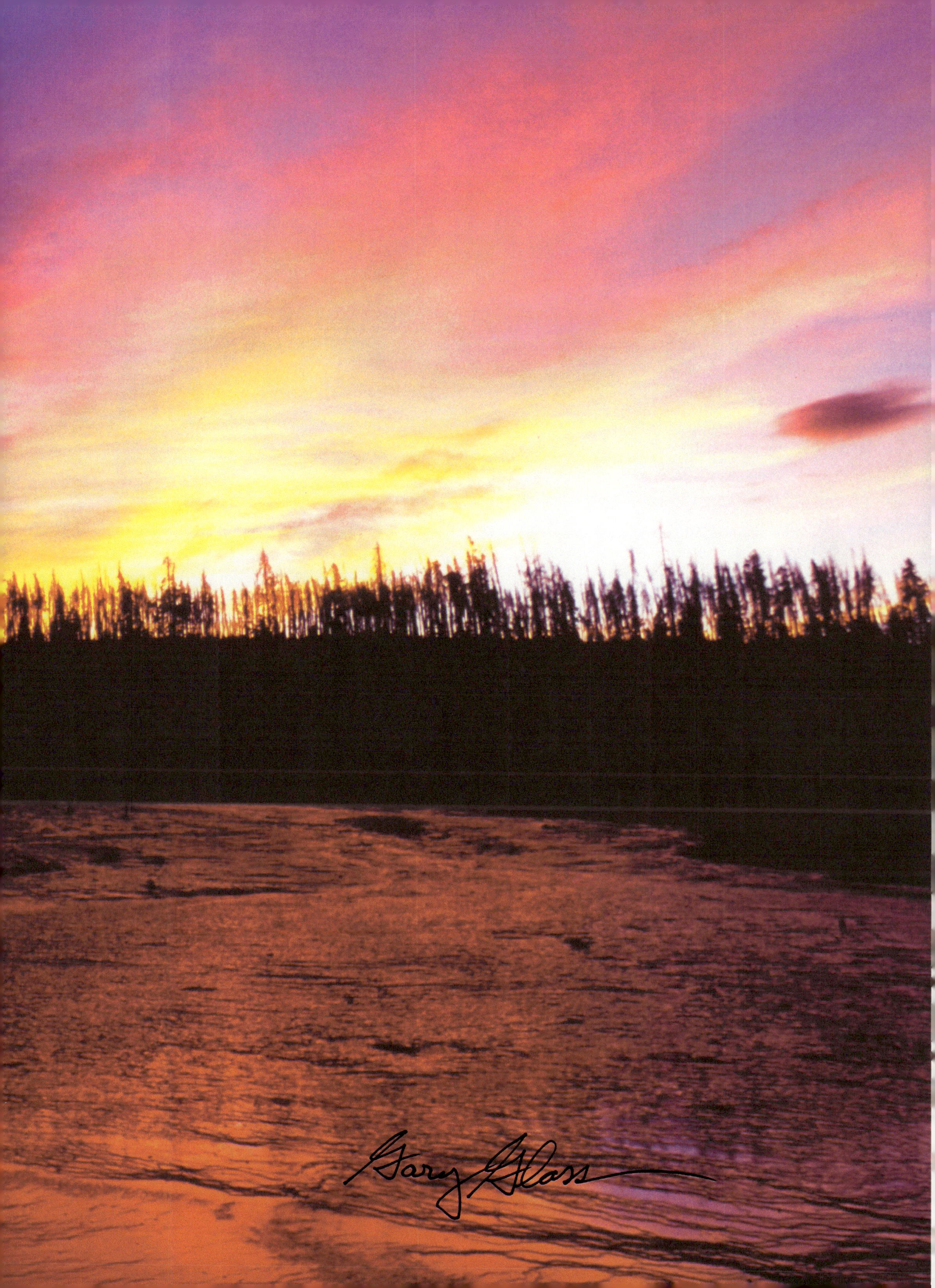
Gary Glass

Minerva Bloom

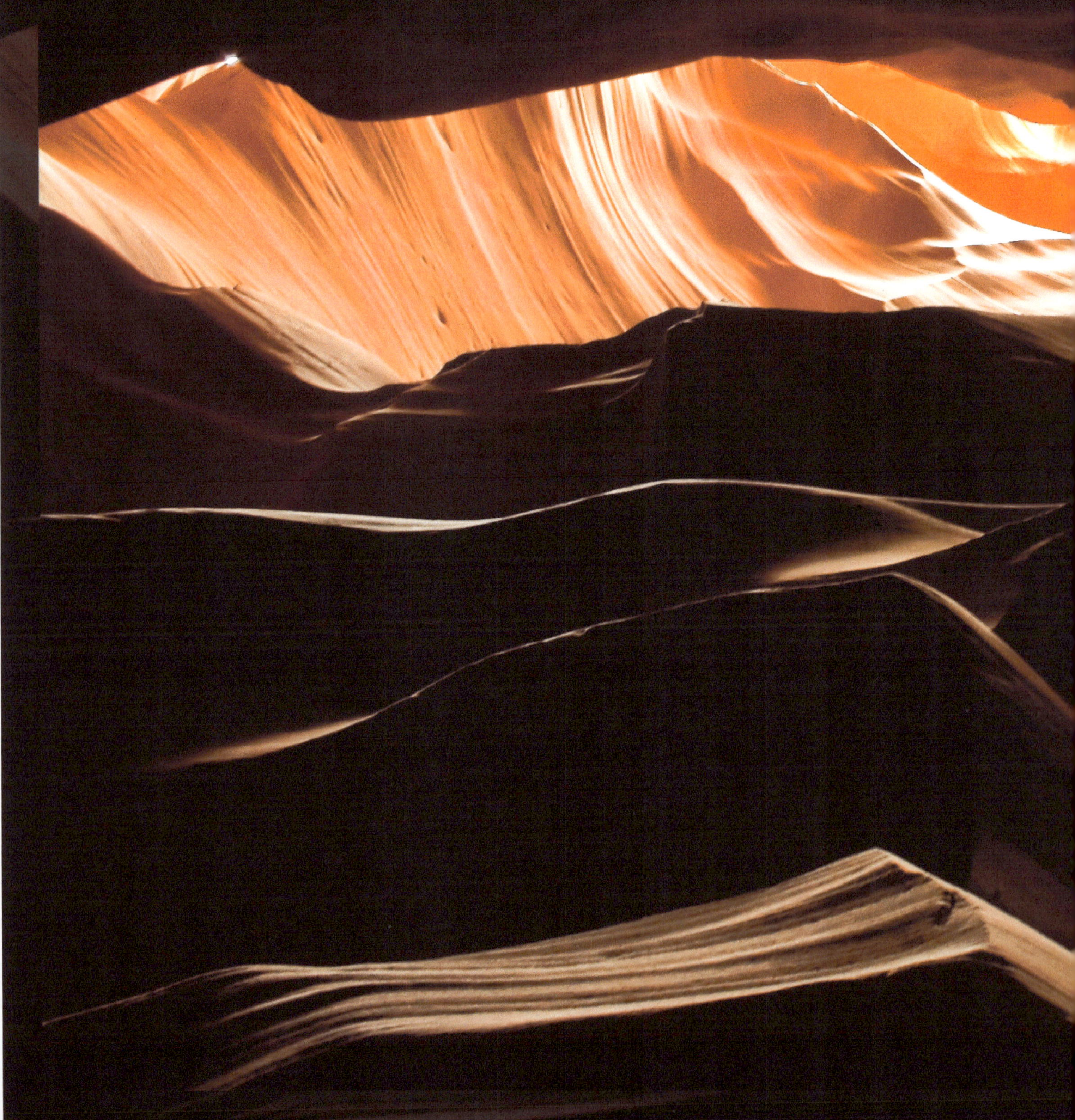

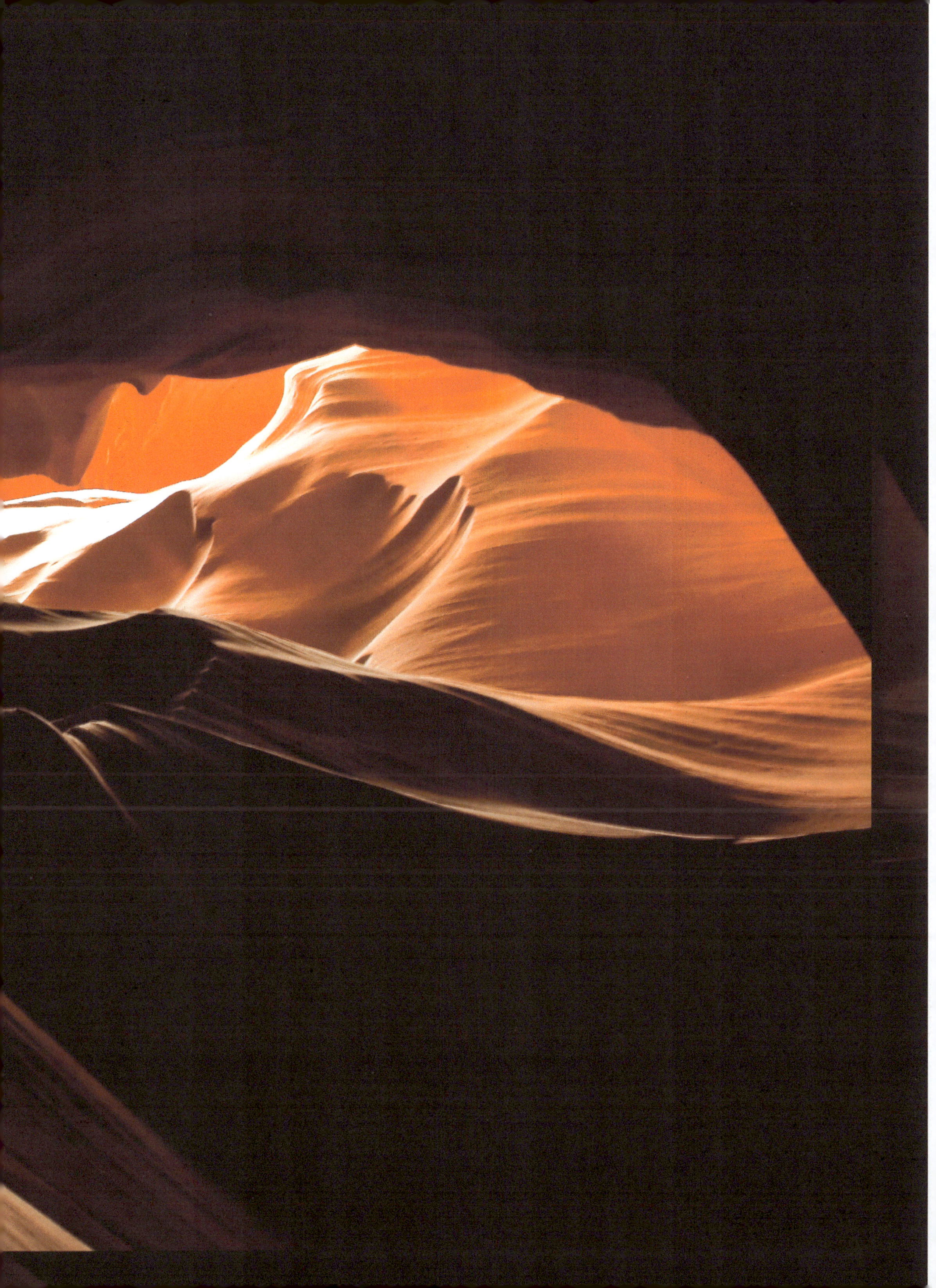

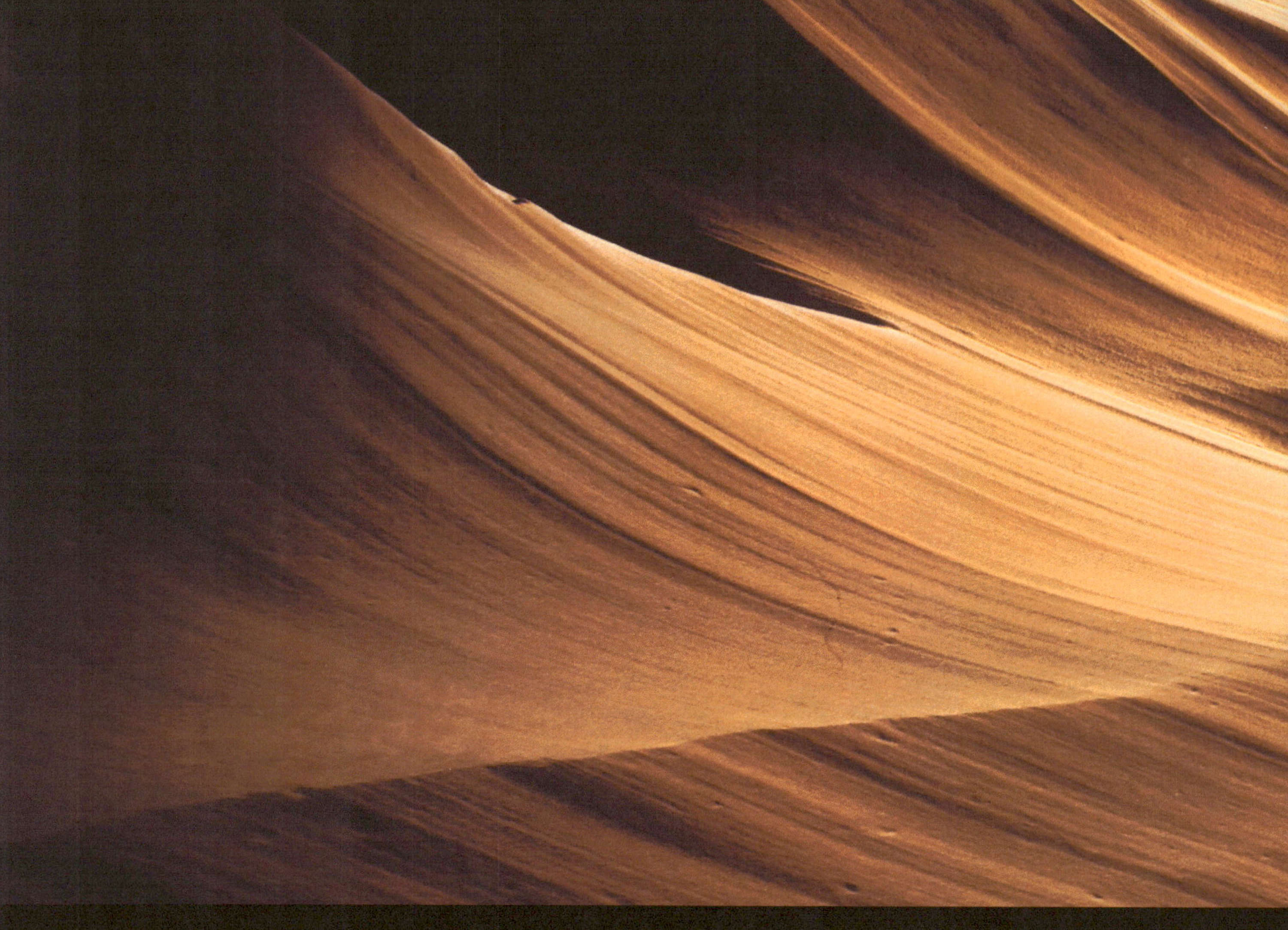

On a visit to the American Southwest, I was rewarded with soul-moving beauty. I immersed myself in the fundamental elements of the desert in a few day's time while exploring some iconic canyons, precipices and towering red buttes.

Several of the locations were difficult to photograph as the constantly shifting and harsh landscape presented some limitations for me. I traveled with a tripod but in some instances, I found it useless due to strong winds, lashing sand or crowds. It is within these limitations that I have learned to improvise when I must: I hold my breath for a few seconds, brace myself, then take a hand-held photograph mindful of the composition angle and light. At other times, I'm caught in the rain or there are overcast skies but I still see a composition. As a result, I'm getting better at doing photography-on-the-fly.

The Antelope Canyon or Tse' bighanilini which means in Navajo "the place where water runs through rocks", is an extremely beautiful place with just the right combination of depth, width, length, rock color and ambient light. The graceful curves of the canyon were created by water and wind, wearing away the sandstone grain by grain. We reached the upper canyon at the end of a very sandy 2 mile 4WD track at midday, when it is known to be the best time to photograph. Photography within slot canyons is difficult due to the wide exposure range (often 10

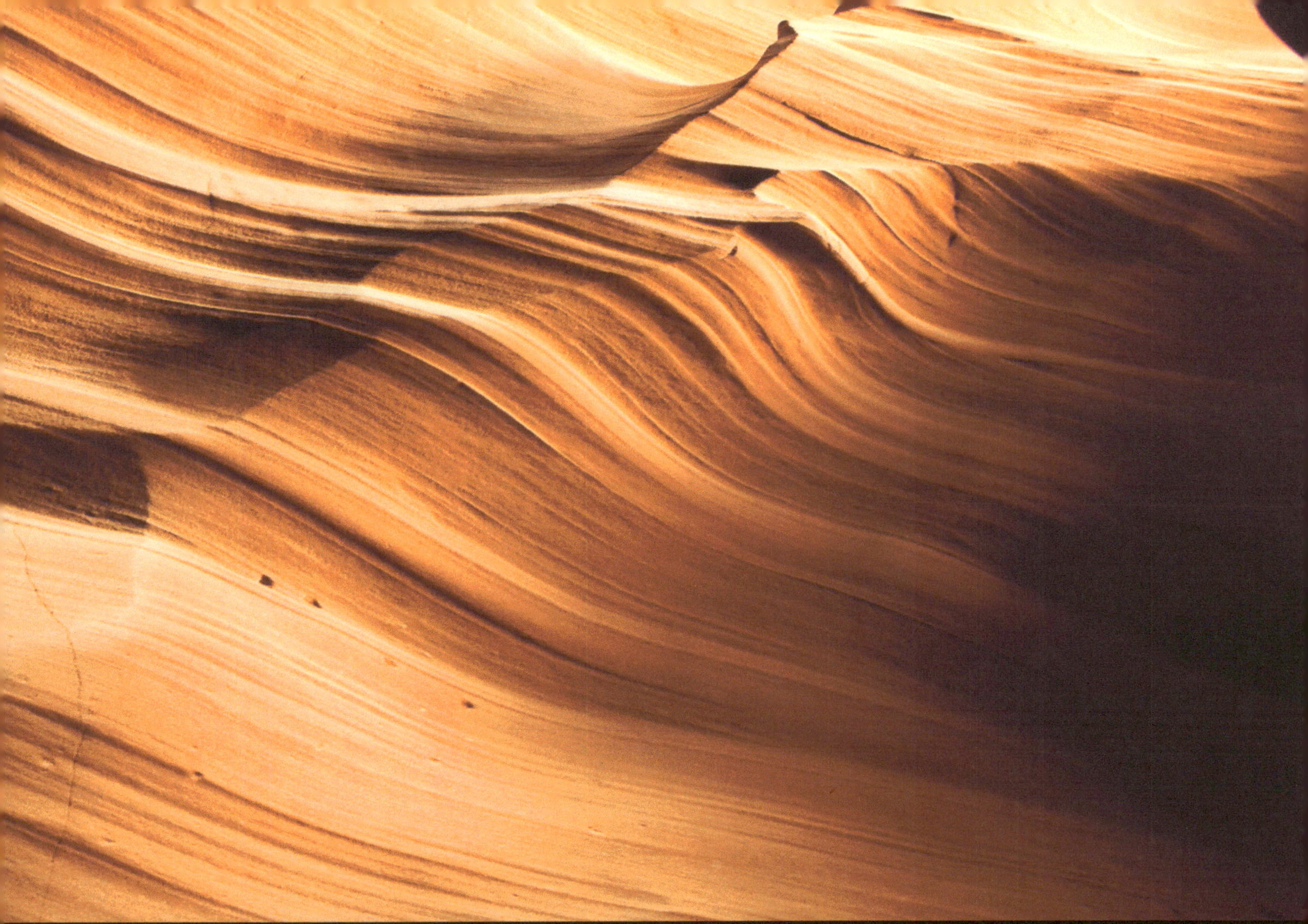

EV or more) made by light reflecting off the canyon walls. Gary Glass, an experienced photographer, passed along several tips for me to practice beforehand with bracket exposures, metering, ISO and minimal aperture combinations and mirror lock-up. There were dozens of people going through the slots with their authorized Navajo guides. The guides didn't want people to linger too long in the corridors. I wasn't able to use a tripod and I found the crowds distracting but I blocked all noises out, supported myself against the rocks and was able to get in the zone to tune into the shapes of the canyon's smooth undulating sandstone.

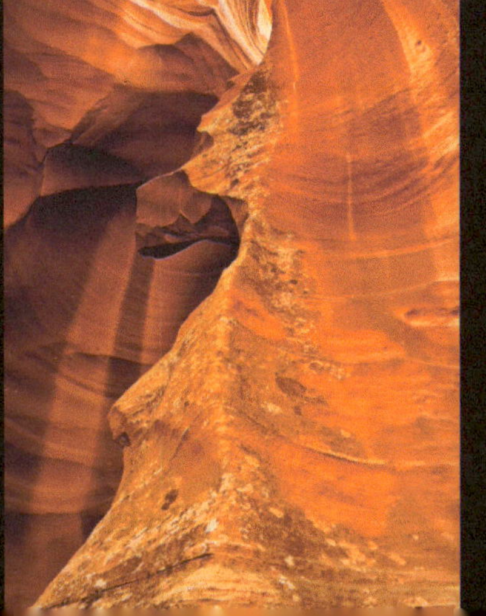

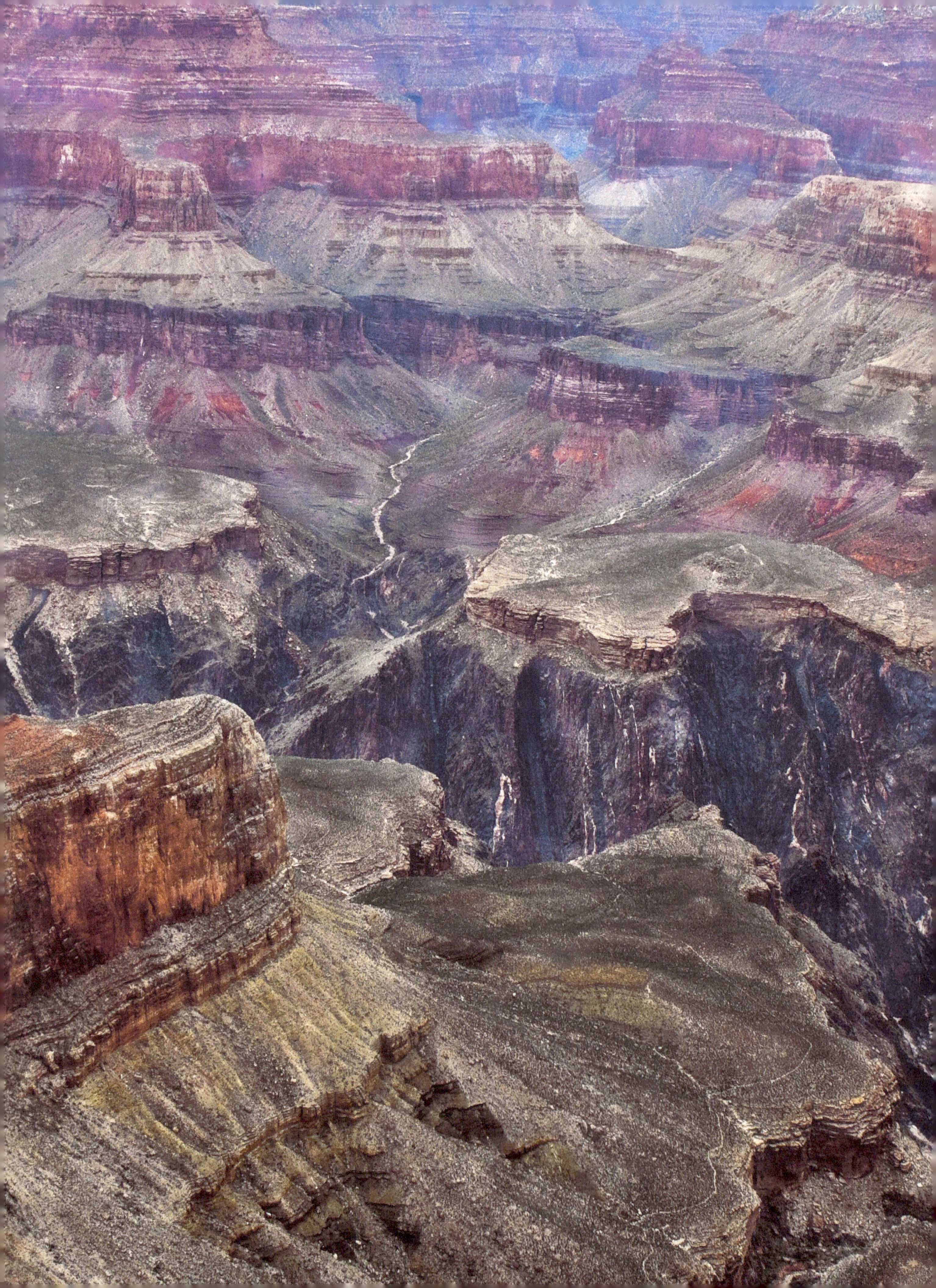

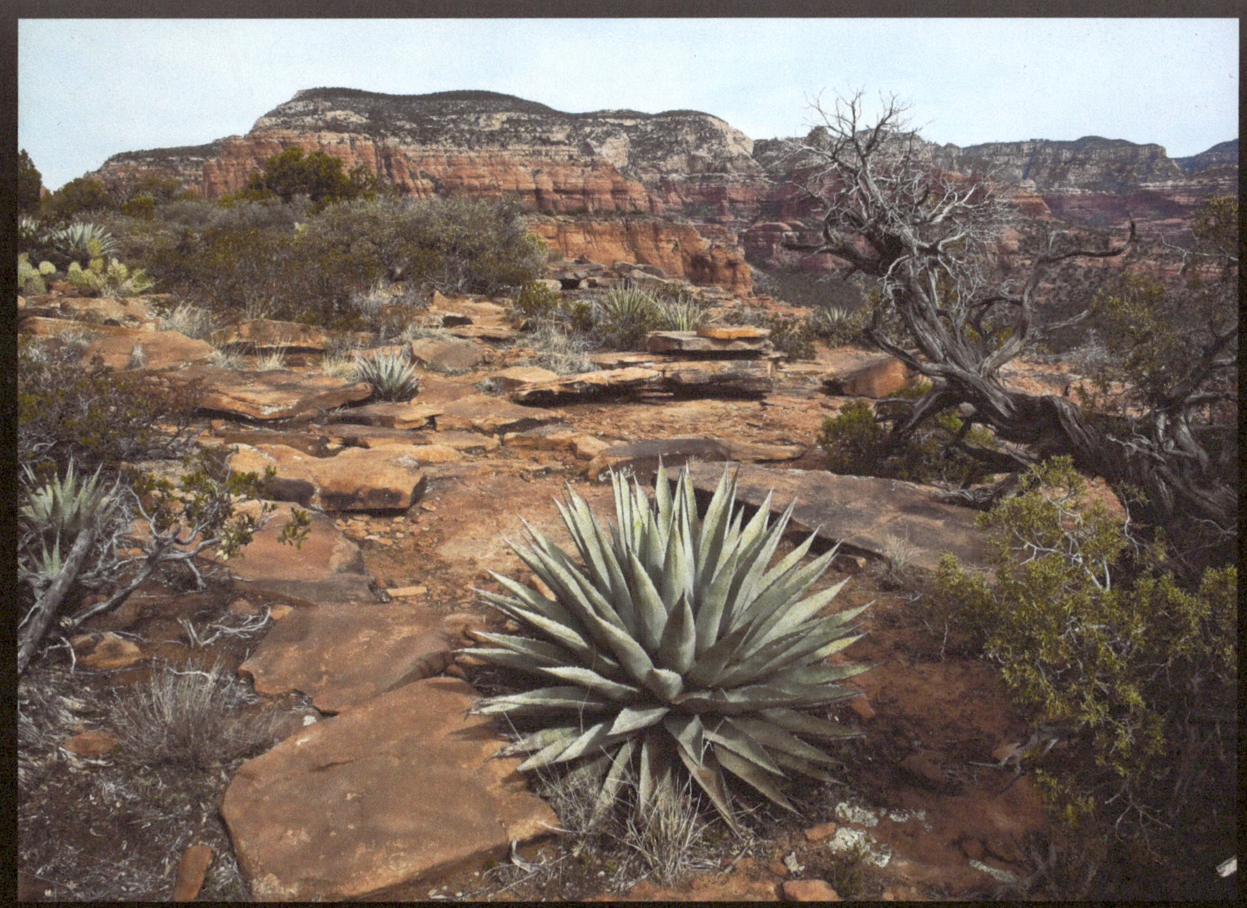

Doe Mountain in Sedona, Arizona is a geologist's dream. Sheer orange cliffs surround the flat-topped mesa, broken slabs of sandstone, striated bluffs and layers of twisted rock are visible everywhere. Not many people know of this mesa. The trail to the top clings to the side of the mountain, and takes you around several switchbacks. It's a moderate 2.6 miles round trip. The entire perimeter consists of a wide, bare, rocky ledge, giving you endless vantage panoramic views of Sedona. When I reached the top of the mesa, I made sure to follow the small visible trails as to not disturb the red soil crust. The textures, colors and lines literally took my breath away. I think I captured a tiny part of that feeling with this image.

Opposite page:
After walking from Yaki Point along the south rim trail, we came to this spot that encircles the Abyss and continues towards Pima Point. I have taken many shots of the Grand Canyon with the horizon in view and this time I wanted to try something different. I found Mohave Point to be with fewer visitors so it's generally more peaceful and it has several individual overlooks rather than just one. It's also the area where Trinity Creek joins the Colorado River. I positioned myself close to the rim and immediately felt the familiar drop in my stomach. A plummeting sensation 3,000 feet deep at this particular point in the canyon. I moved away from the horizon and zoomed into the layered earth to find an organic abstract of vermillion, lavender-browns, gray, black and cream colors of sandstone, limestone and shale shaping the canyon walls.

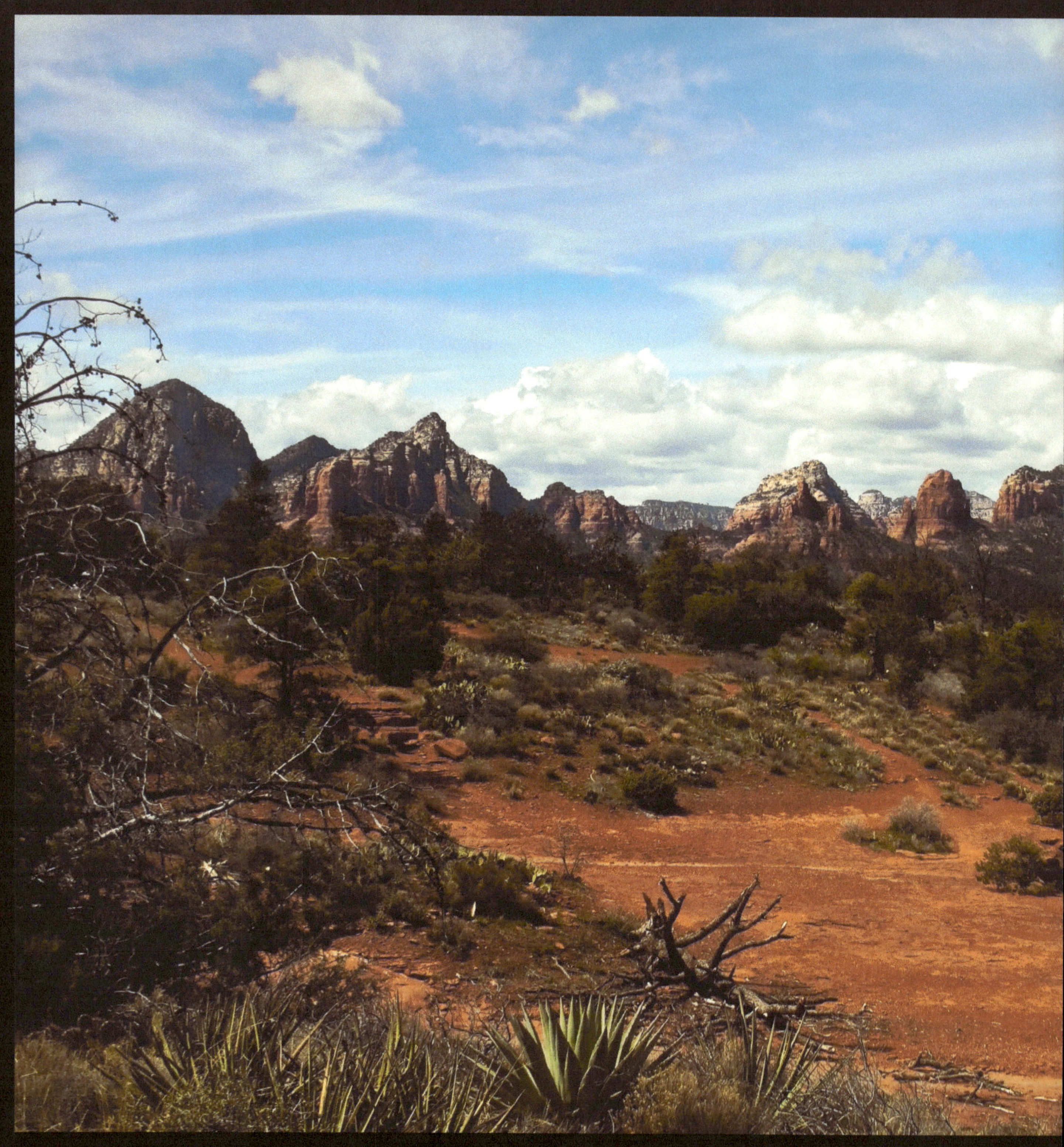

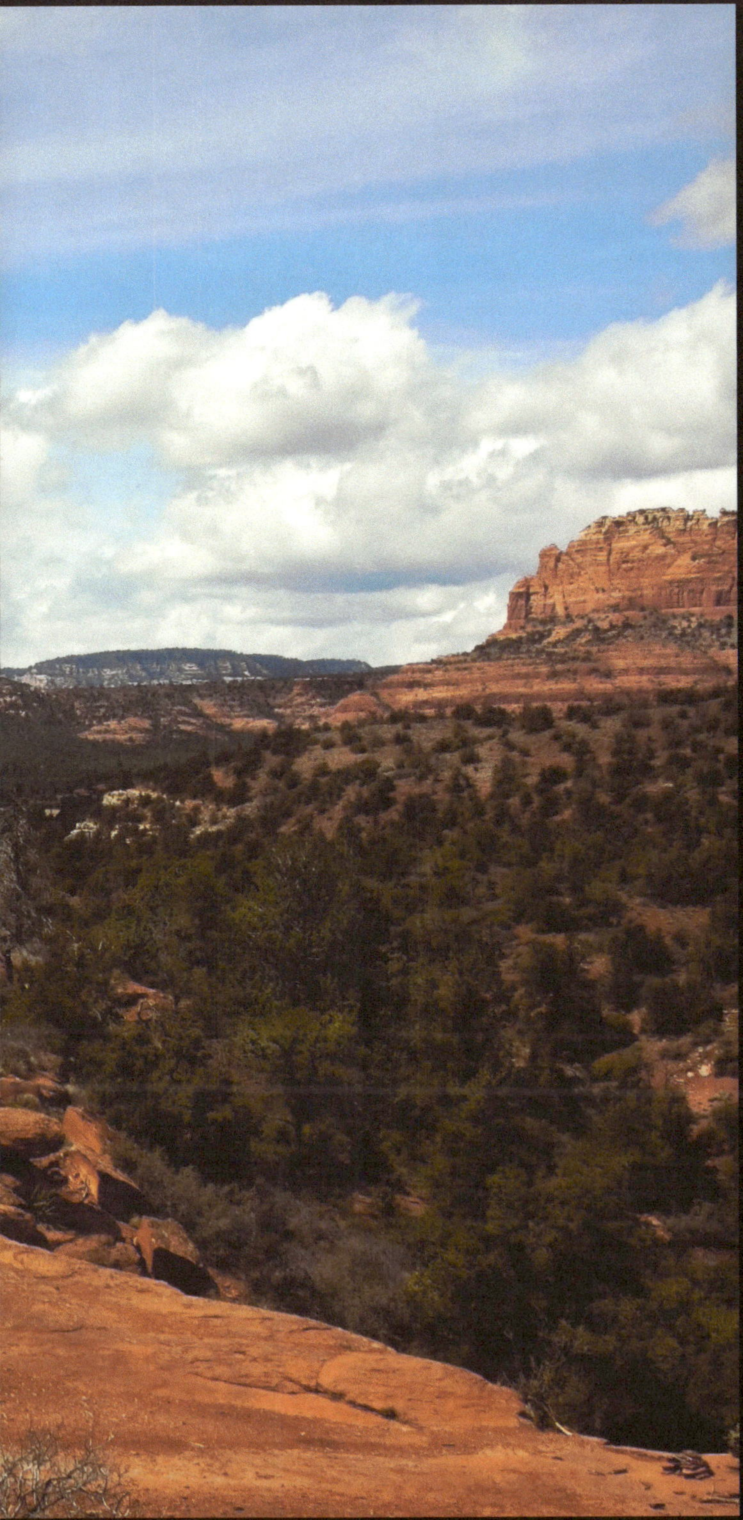

Sedona, is a very unique place on earth, one of my favorites. A place of crossroads and contrasts as it marks the edge of ancient seas. A place of crisp blue skies, greens of every hue, reds and golds and also colors from the softest peach to the deepest vermillion. The climate varies from canyon, to creekside, to slope and the terrain hosts a myriad habitats for plants and animals. The area is a lesson in time, because over the course of millions of years the sea and the desert intersected to produce a complex mosaic of geologic forms as vibrant as a painter's palette. I took this panoramic image from the Schnebly Hill area, in an effort to represent my sensory perceptions of Sedona.

Below:
Cathedral Rock winter scene.

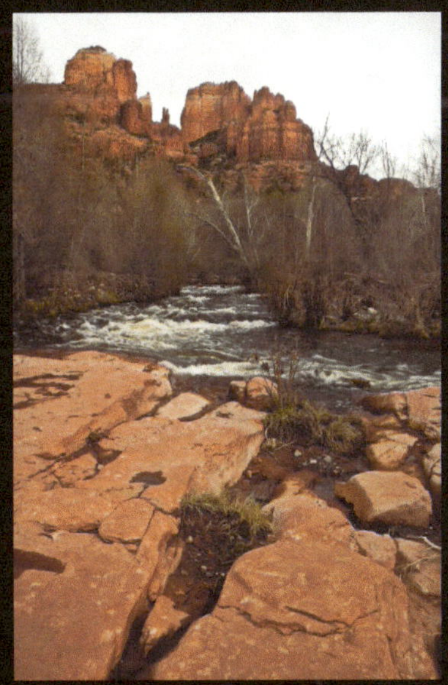

During a week-long visit to North Carolina, my husband and I drove through the Blue Ridge Parkway and made several stops to explore some nature trails. It was an early morning when we began hiking the Waterrock Knob trail (MP 451.2) and the fog from the previous evening was still lingering in the forest. The scattered light and texture gave a moody atmospheric feel at 6200 feet elevation. I stopped for a moment to enjoy the surroundings and when I turned around I saw this composition. I decided to go for a short exposure to prevent the fog from smoothing out, since the fog was moving rather quickly at this point.

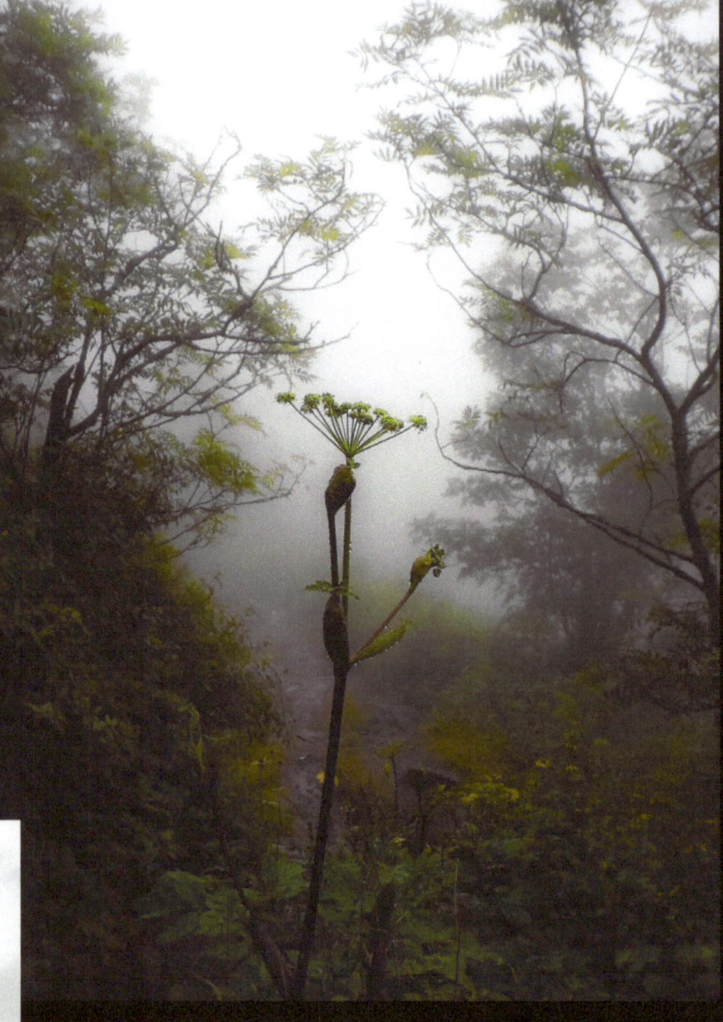

On the following day, we woke up to a view of rising, swirling fog, as it began forming in the Appalachian mountains. The trees gave me a good frame for contrast.

Later on that week, I decided to take a walk just before sunrise, as I couldn't sleep. I caught this view of silhouettes and mist at Lake Toxaway, in between twilight and the beginning of sunrise.

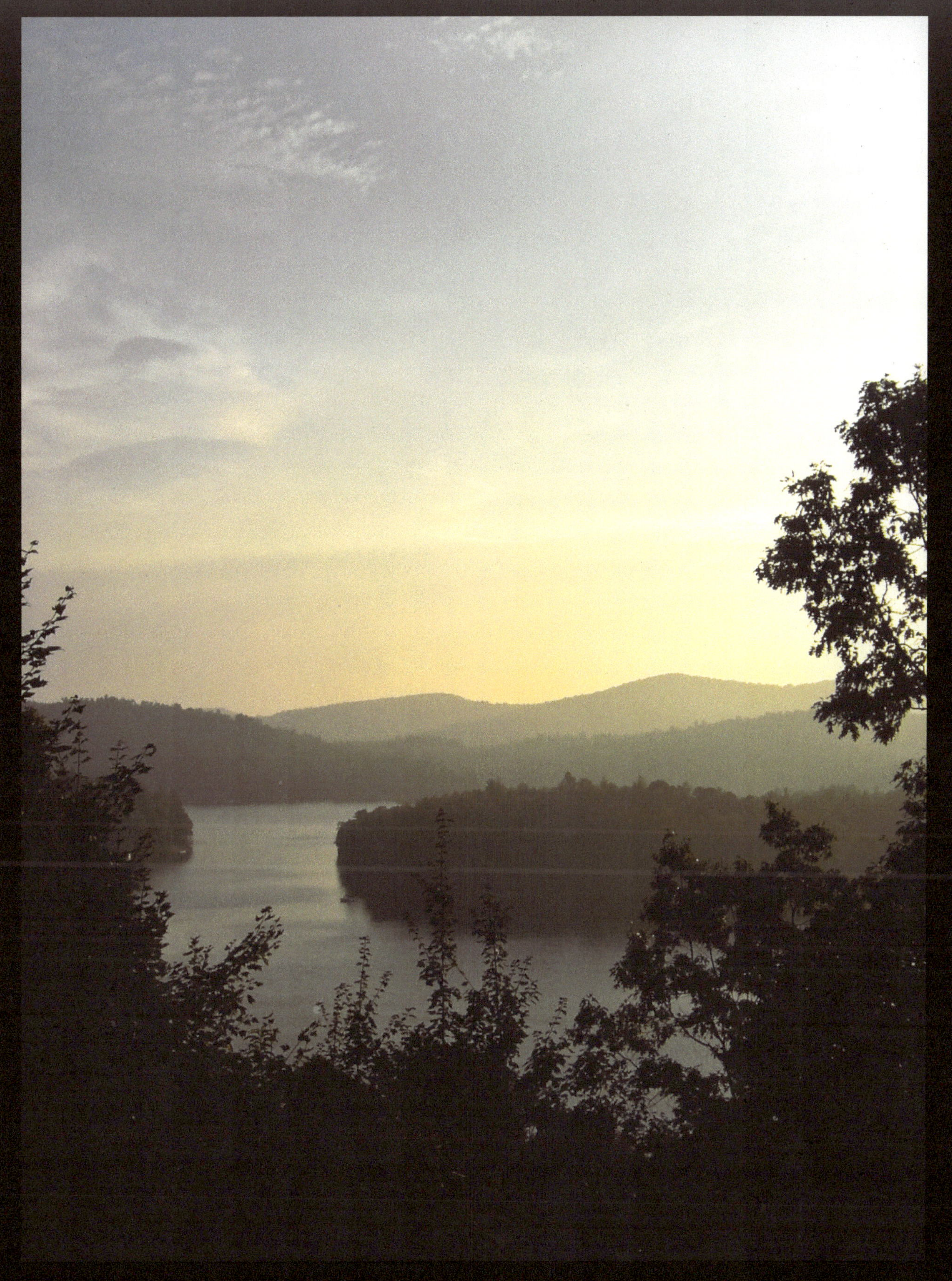

With travel photography you have to work with sub-optimal lighting (since you can't plan to see everything during the Golden Hour), and with only so much time in a place, you end up going to some gorgeous places during the wrong time of the day and you have to try to get the best shot you can with what light there is.

Another challenge is trying to take pictures while traveling companions or tour guides insist that you rush through everything at breakneck speed and then learning to navigate oblivious bystanders.

Within the Vermillion Cliffs area in Page, Arizona lies the Glen Canyon, carved by the Colorado River. The early stages of sunset were illuminating the canyon walls with golden tones. It was very windy, sand was whipping at my face and I was worried about my camera, but I couldn't pass this shot. I secured myself in a large rock and sat by the cliff's edge overlooking the flowing river, in an area below the Glen Canyon dam. There was a light haze in the horizon, so instead, aware of depth of field, I framed a composition within the glowing canyon walls and the river— which surface was rippling from the lashing wind. This is a hand-held shot.

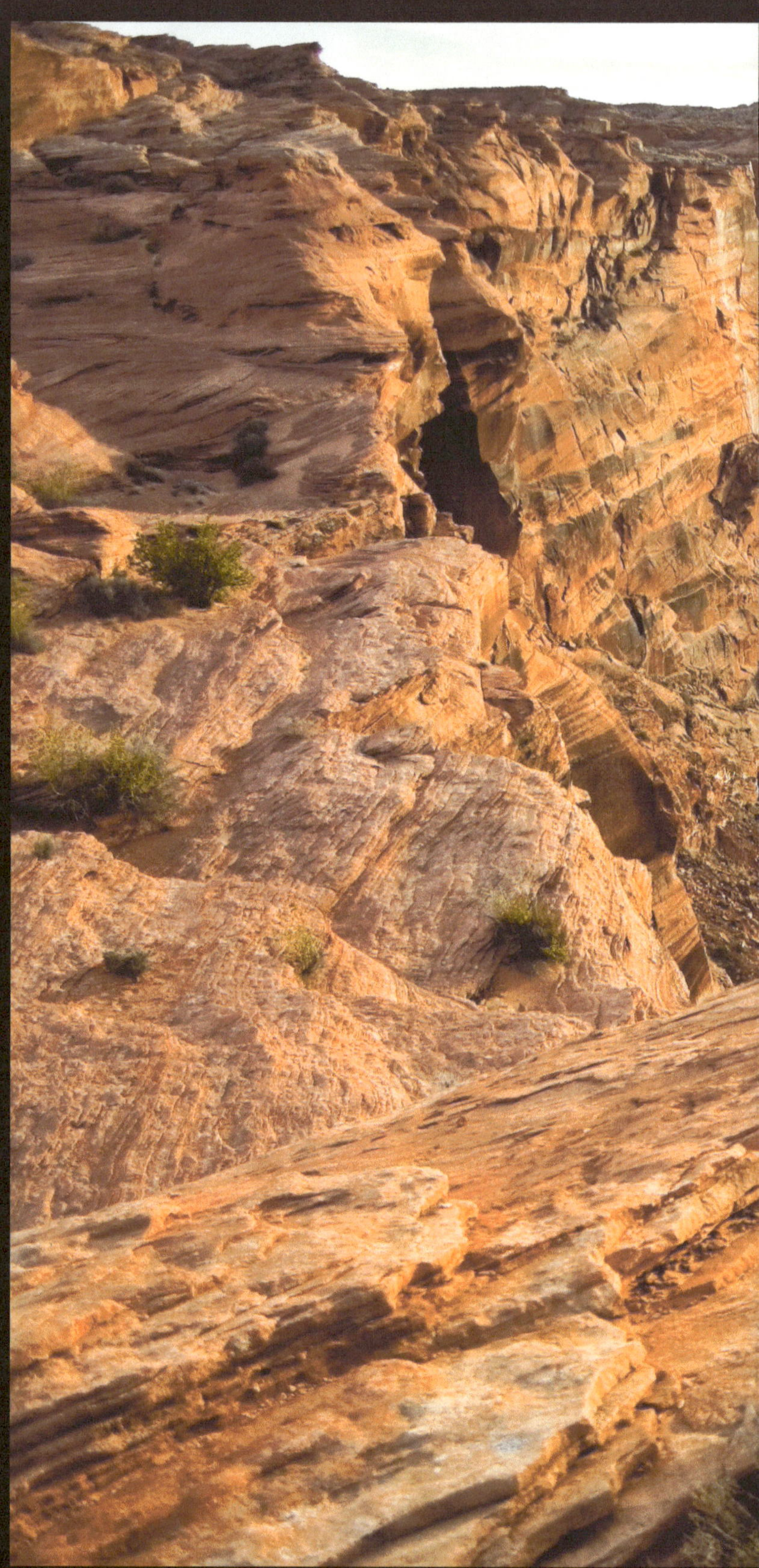

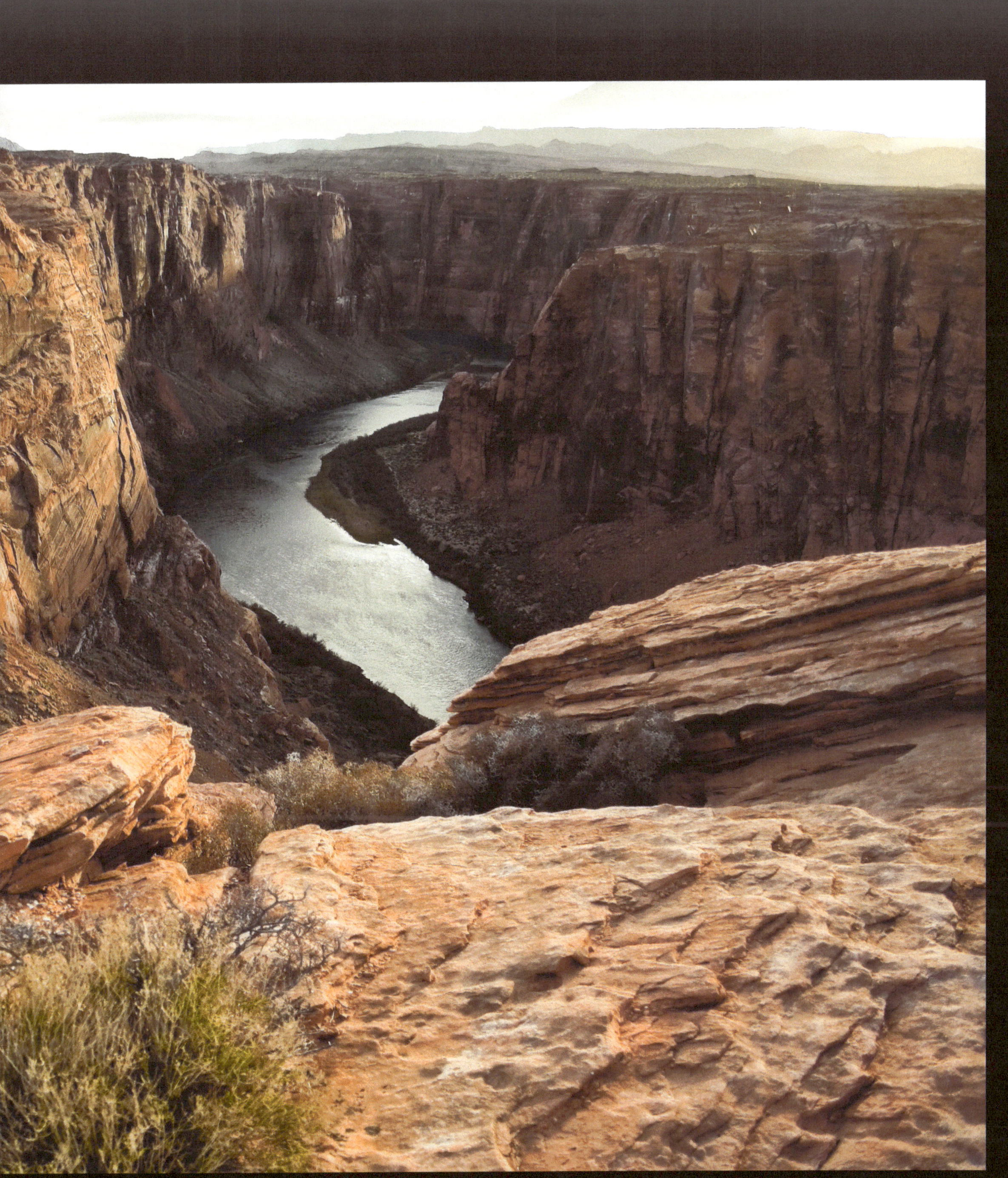

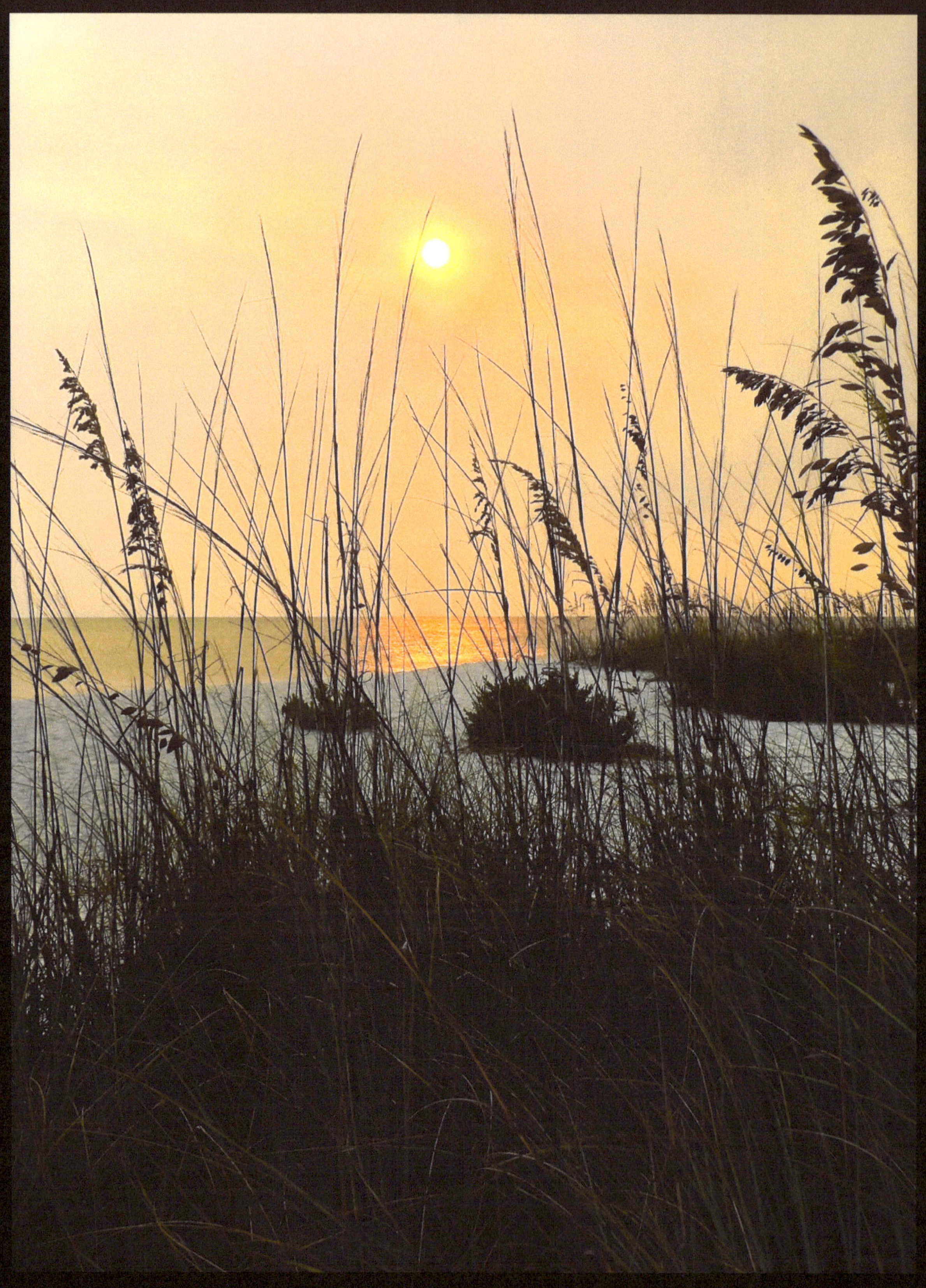

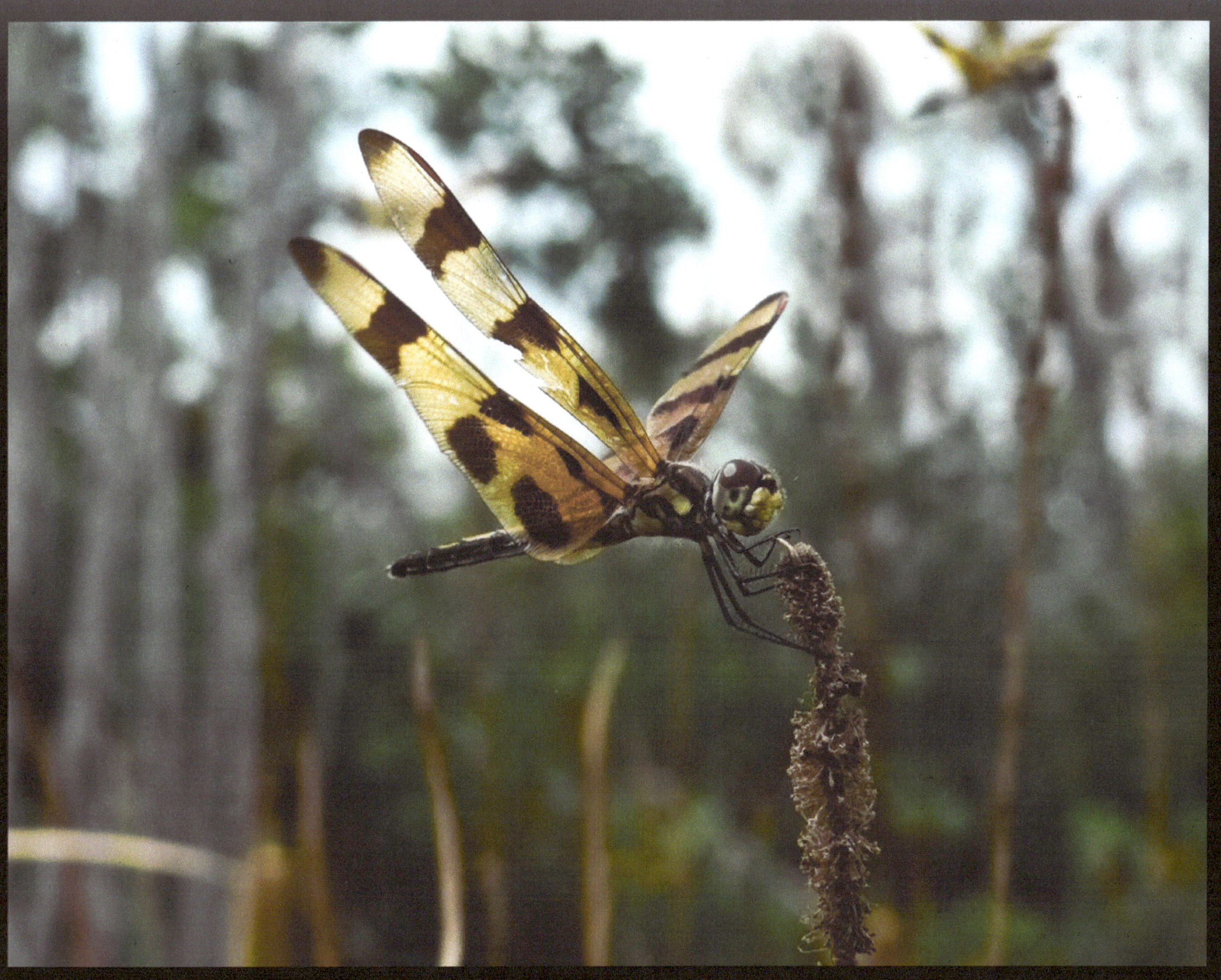

While walking along a beach trail in Sanibel Island, I came upon a Halloween Pennant dragonfly by the banks of a creek. Dragonflies were always a source of wonder for me as a child. This one was busily eating from a field of cattails. There were many more dragonflies buzzing around and they didn't mind my presence so I was delighted to take pictures while they munched away. About 75% of Sanibel Island is a wildlife preserve, so finding dragonflies was not very difficult. This Island is a breeding ground for these insects as there are wetlands, bays, bayous, creeks and rivers throughout.

Opposite Page:
Later on that afternoon, despite the haze, I caught a sunset reflection with pastel colored hues, at Bowman's Beach through a little path in the dunes.

In the area of San Diego, California, the Torrey Pines State Natural Reserve is a wilderness island in an urban sea. The Reserve is a fragile environment, home to the nation's rarest pine tree: the Torrey pine—which grows only here and on Santa Rosa Island. In December 2009, the area received several inches of rain after a long dry spell. Erosion plays a big part in shaping this coastal land, and we became aware of this fact, on our second visit to the Reserve.

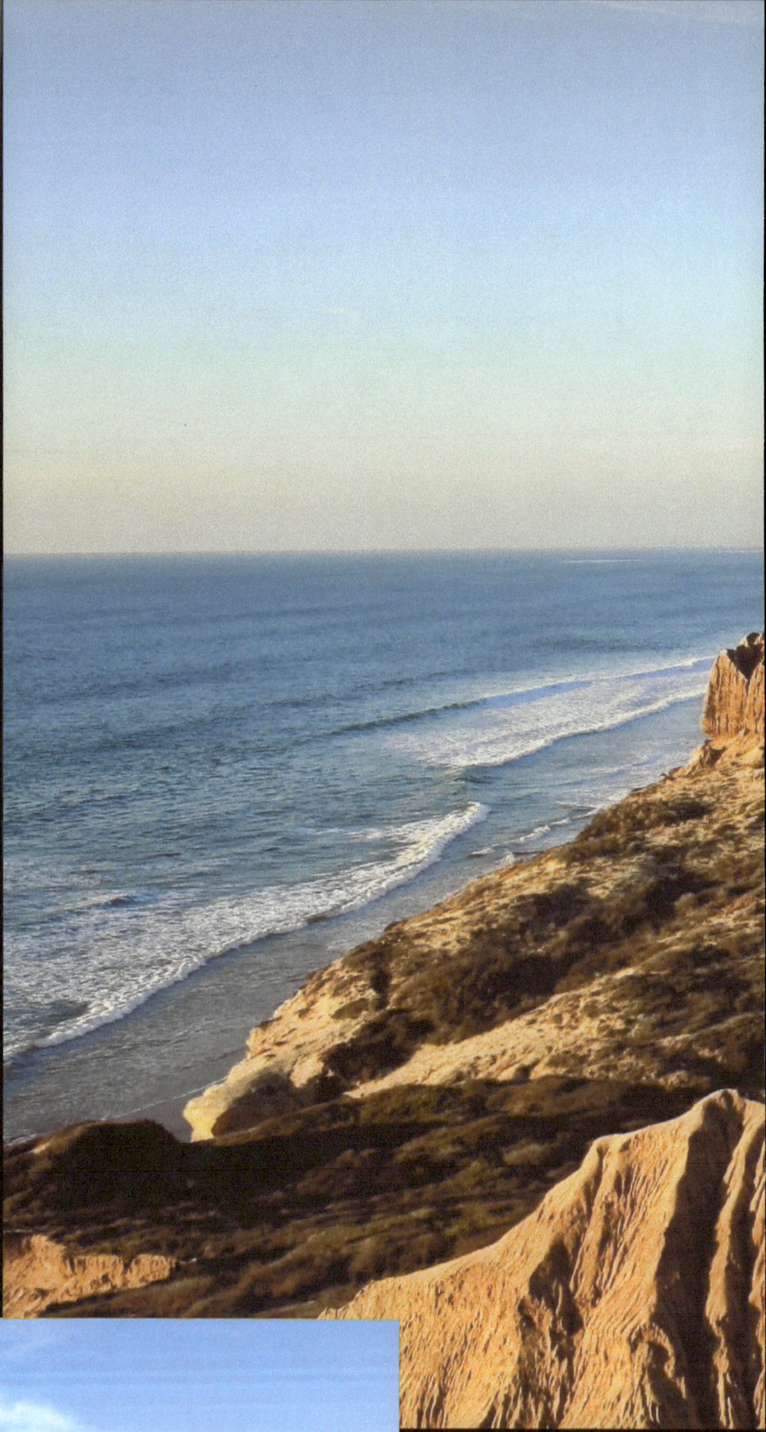

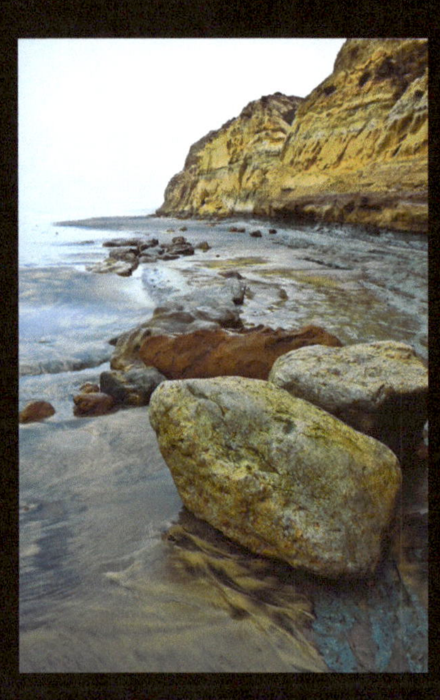

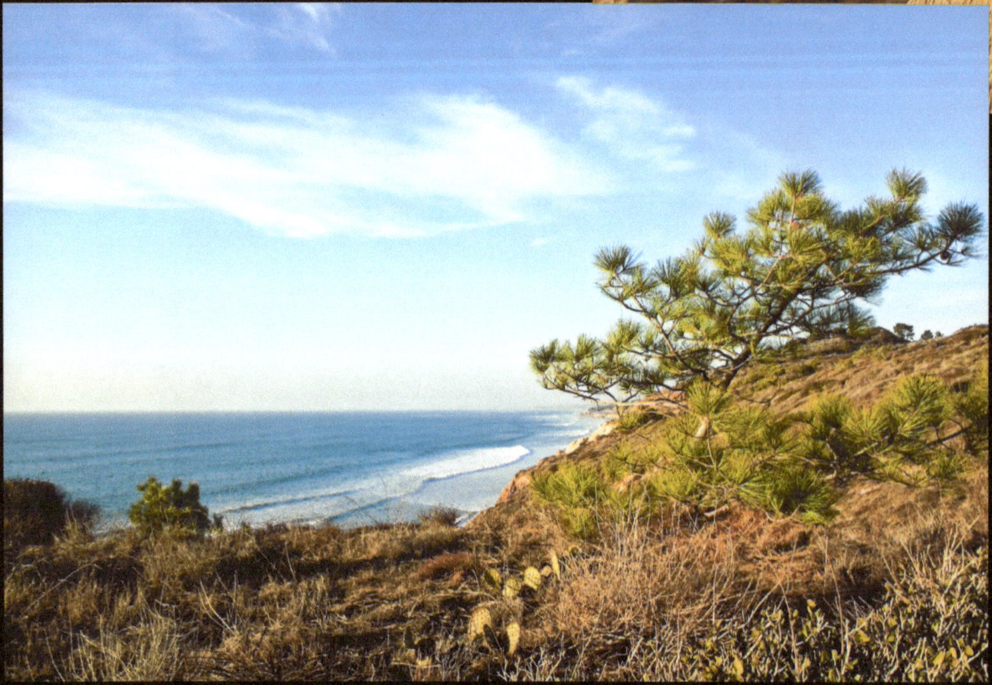

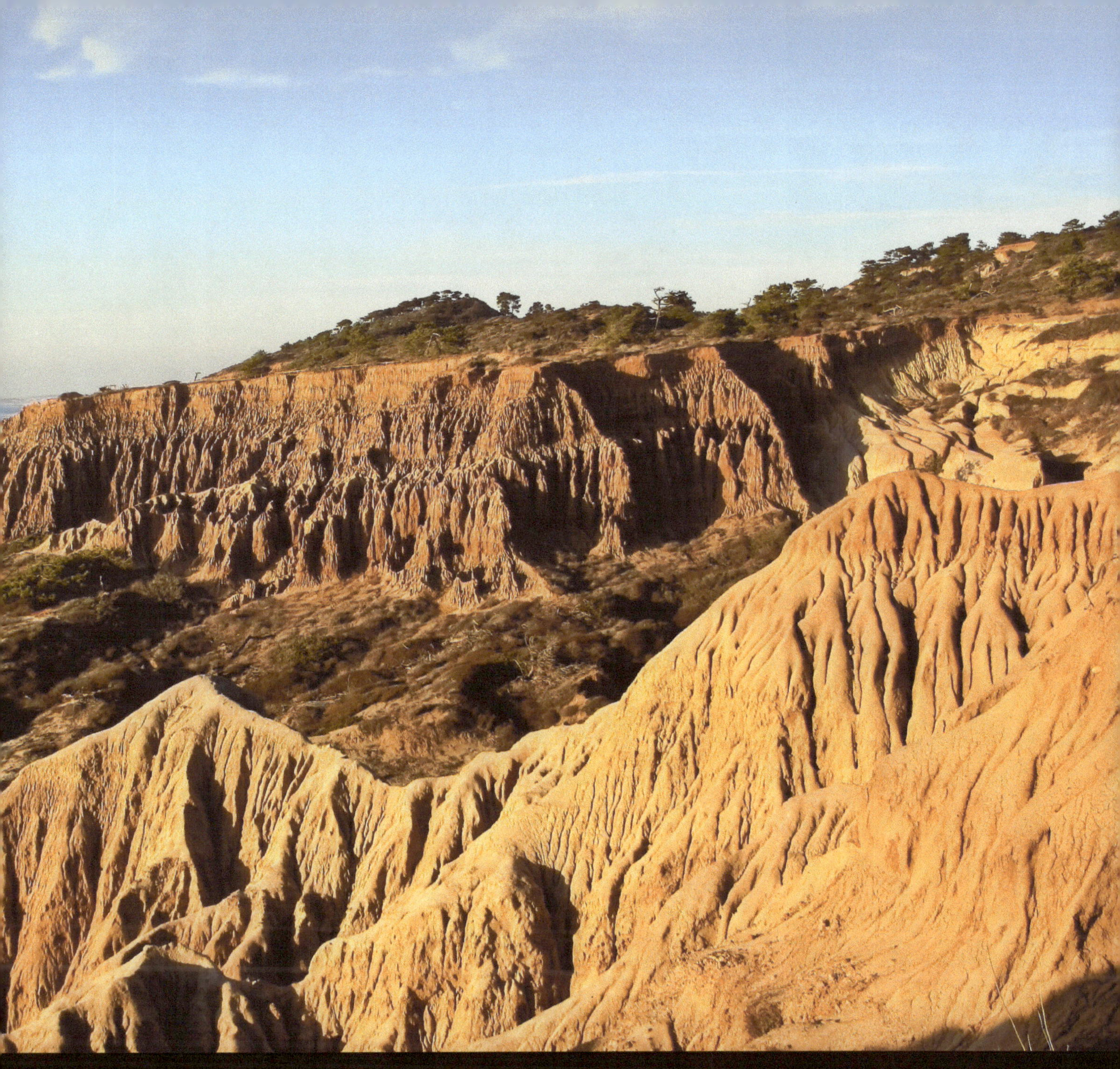

From one day to the other, the natural physical features of the trails had changed. The cliffs and deep ravines of the headlands were crumbling down into the Canyon of the Swifts and the earth was shifting by the hour. The park rangers were forced to close several trails, due to mudslides as the rainwater settled in on the parched land. I took these images at Torrey Pines on two consecutive days. I dealt with fog and rain on the first day, despite that, I made the ¾ mile trail descent to the beach. On the second day, some of the trails were cleared and I caught some high ocean views and a wind-sculpted pine, from atop the plateaus at Guy Flemming and Razor Point Trails as the day was weaning down

In Upper Oak Creek Canyon, the West Fork Trail in Sedona, Arizona winds through vertical sandstone cliffs that tower hundreds of feet above the perennial stream. The canyon's floor is shaded by a mix of old-growth ponderosa pine, maples and Douglas fir, as well as stream-side deciduous trees.

The deep, shaded canyon posed a challenge. Metering in such circumstances is the best solution. I measured my shots and checked that the exposure was where I wanted it. If the camera's suggestion was to limit the dynamic range of a composition, then I could pretty much adjust the meter, switch to aperture priority, take a shot and decide where I wanted the exposure to lie from there.

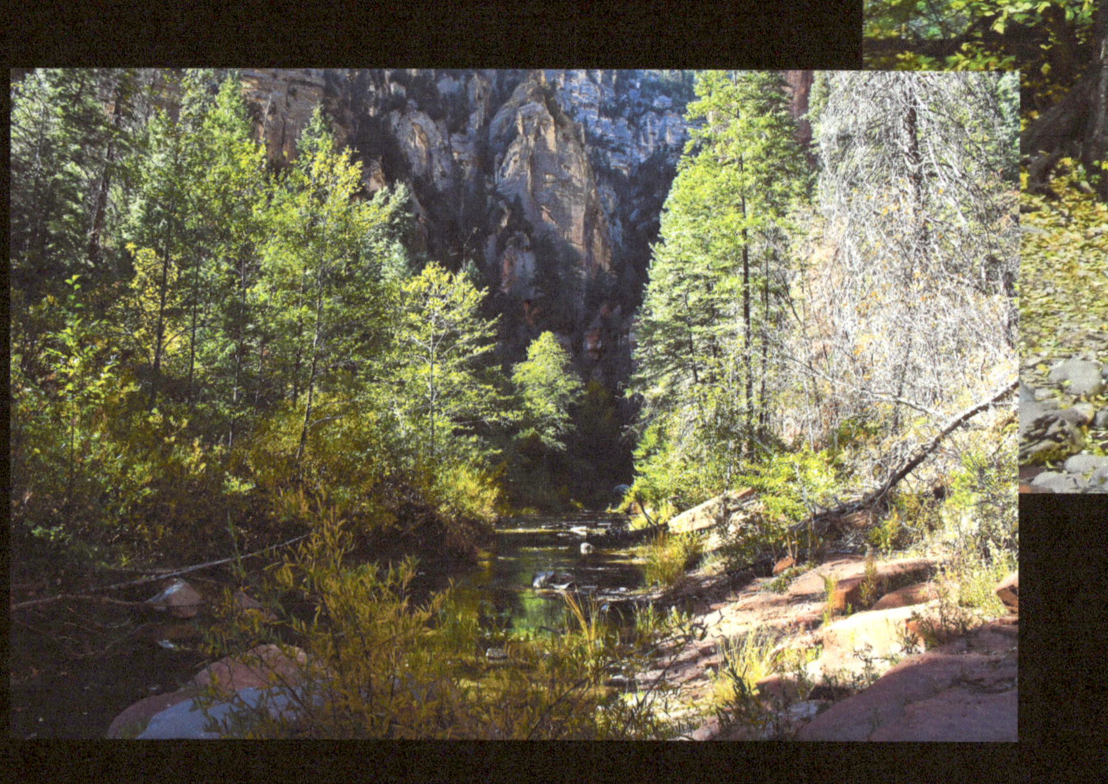

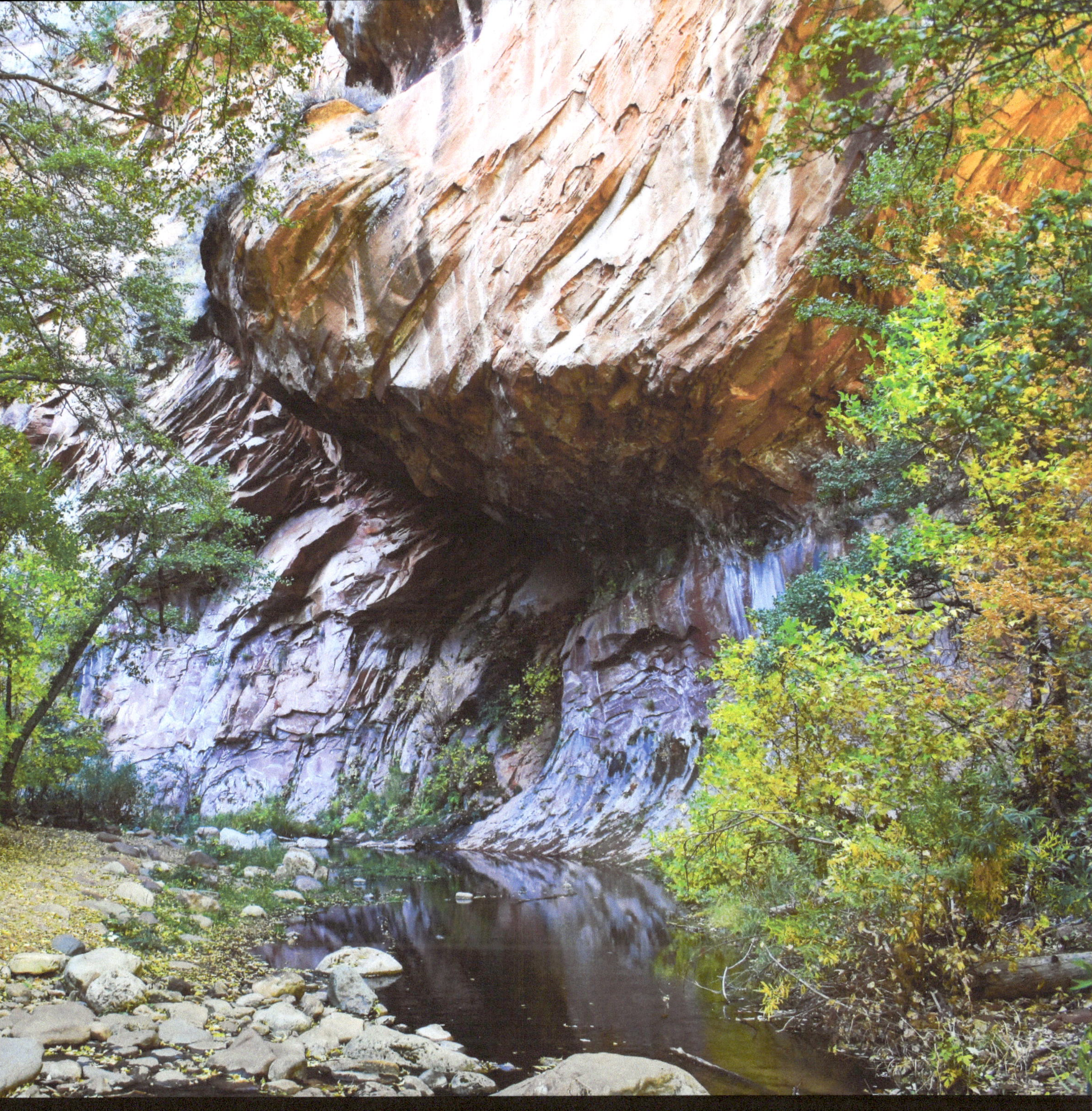

I've been to the creek at different times of the year and my favorite is the autumn season. I was able to explore about 6 miles of the creek during this season. It is best to go on weekdays and in the early mornings when there are less people, but you can easily set up a tripod and linger in the trail as long as you want. It is one of Sedona's premier hikes.

Among La Jolla's cliffs and the scenic California coastline these group of Brown Pelicans were settling down to rest. I walked down the hill to the large grass park at La Jolla Cove to see the pelicans at water level and stood at the base of a low bluff just above the waves. I was careful not to get too close as I didn't want to frighten them, however I'm sure they're used to people mingling about. I had the challenge of mid-morning on an overcast December day as diffused light scattered through the clifftops. The softer light actually made it easier to concentrate on the subjects as opposed to having harsh shadows falling on them.

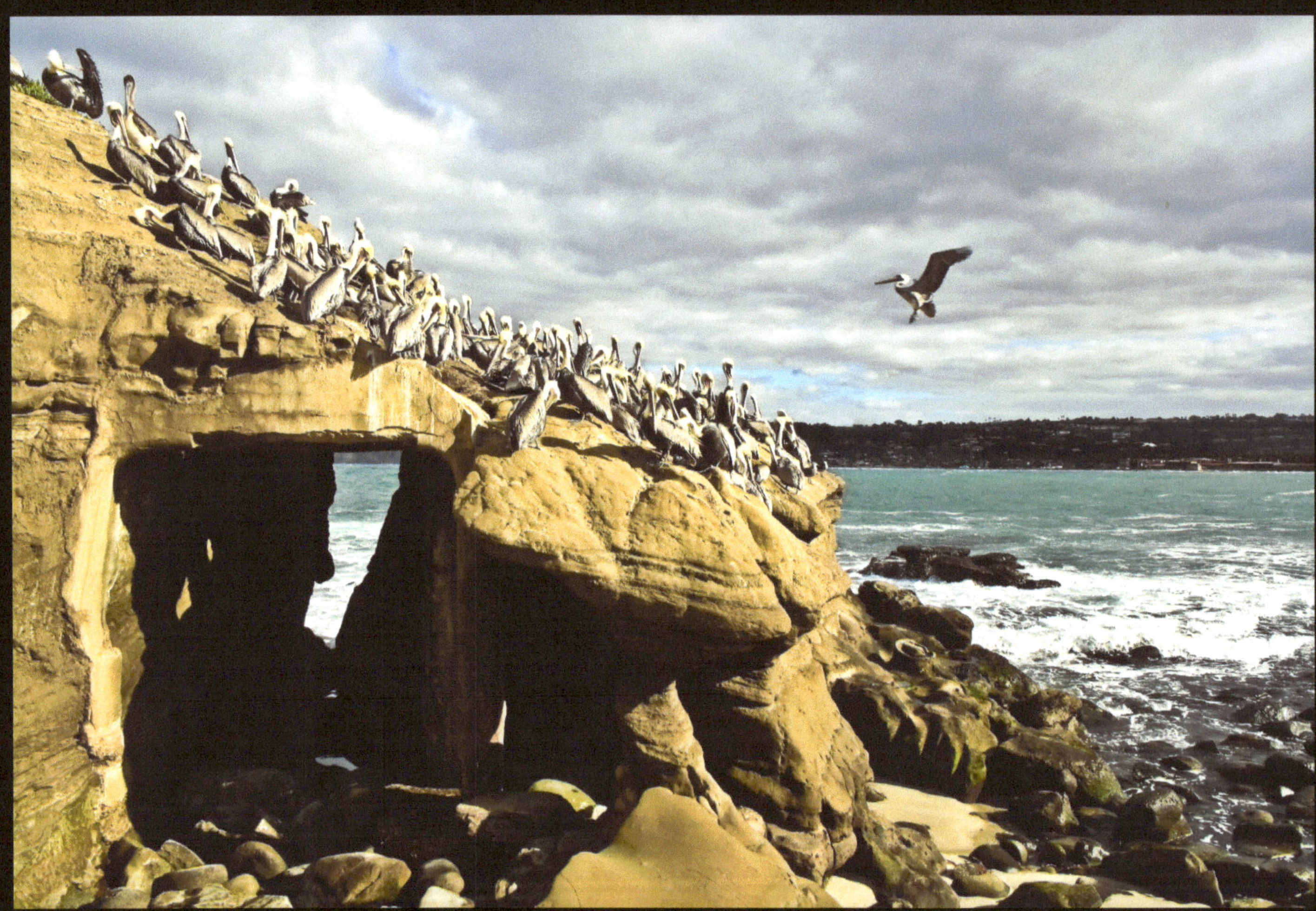

As I keep expanding my journey within the photography field, I will concentrate more and more into landscapes and organic abstracts. I also enjoy the drama and contrast that comes with black and white images. It is a vast field, and I've only scratched the surface. My main goal is to capture the essence of a place, so that years later when I look at the photos, I can feel like I am returning to that place. My equipment slowly keeps on expanding and I'm ever so excited as to what comes next. Time will tell. Doing this book project along with two photographers I admire, has immensely helped me in finding my own voice. That our style and approach is different, is the junction in the Crossroads. We are crossing paths and nature photography is our common bond.

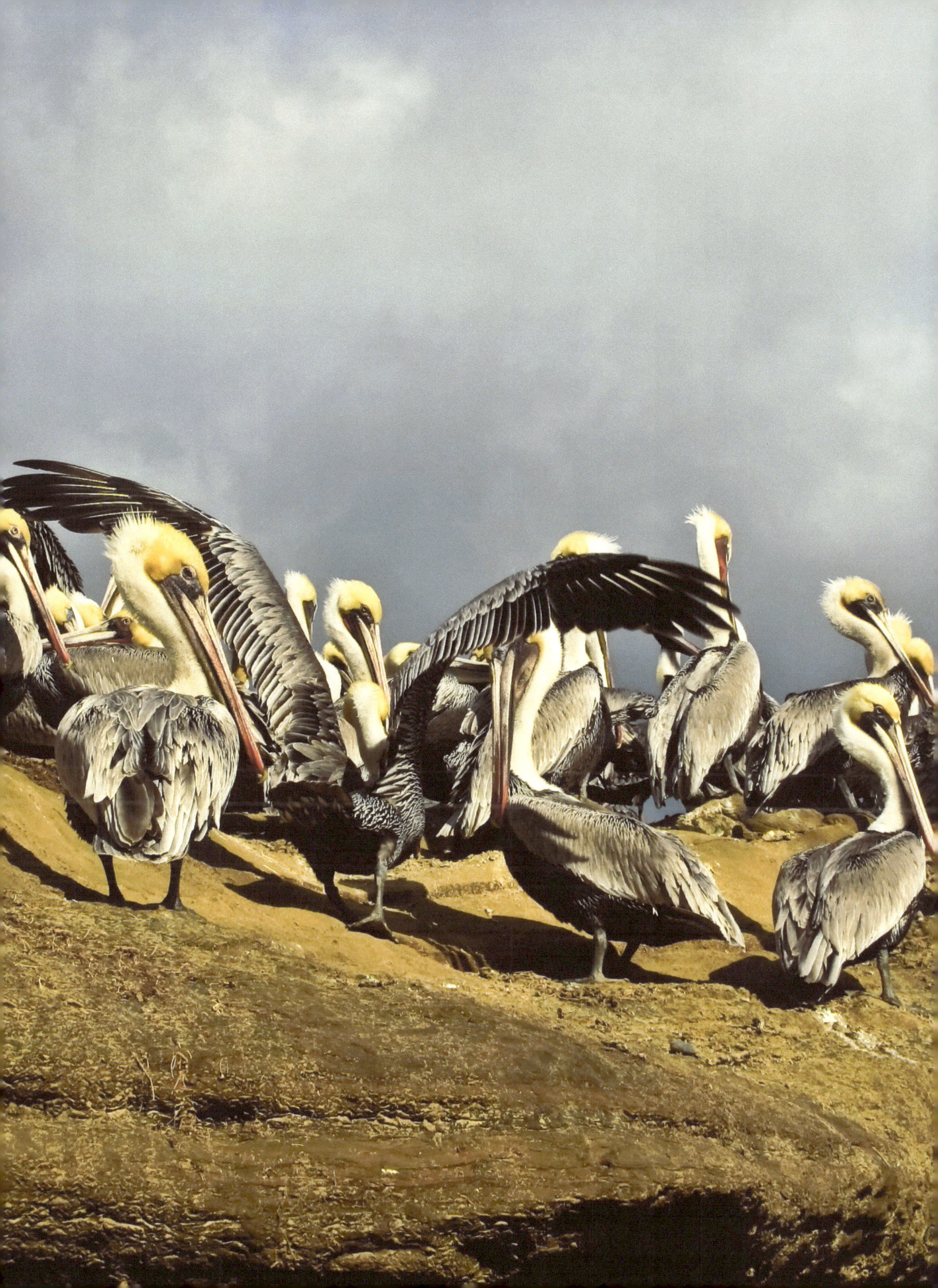

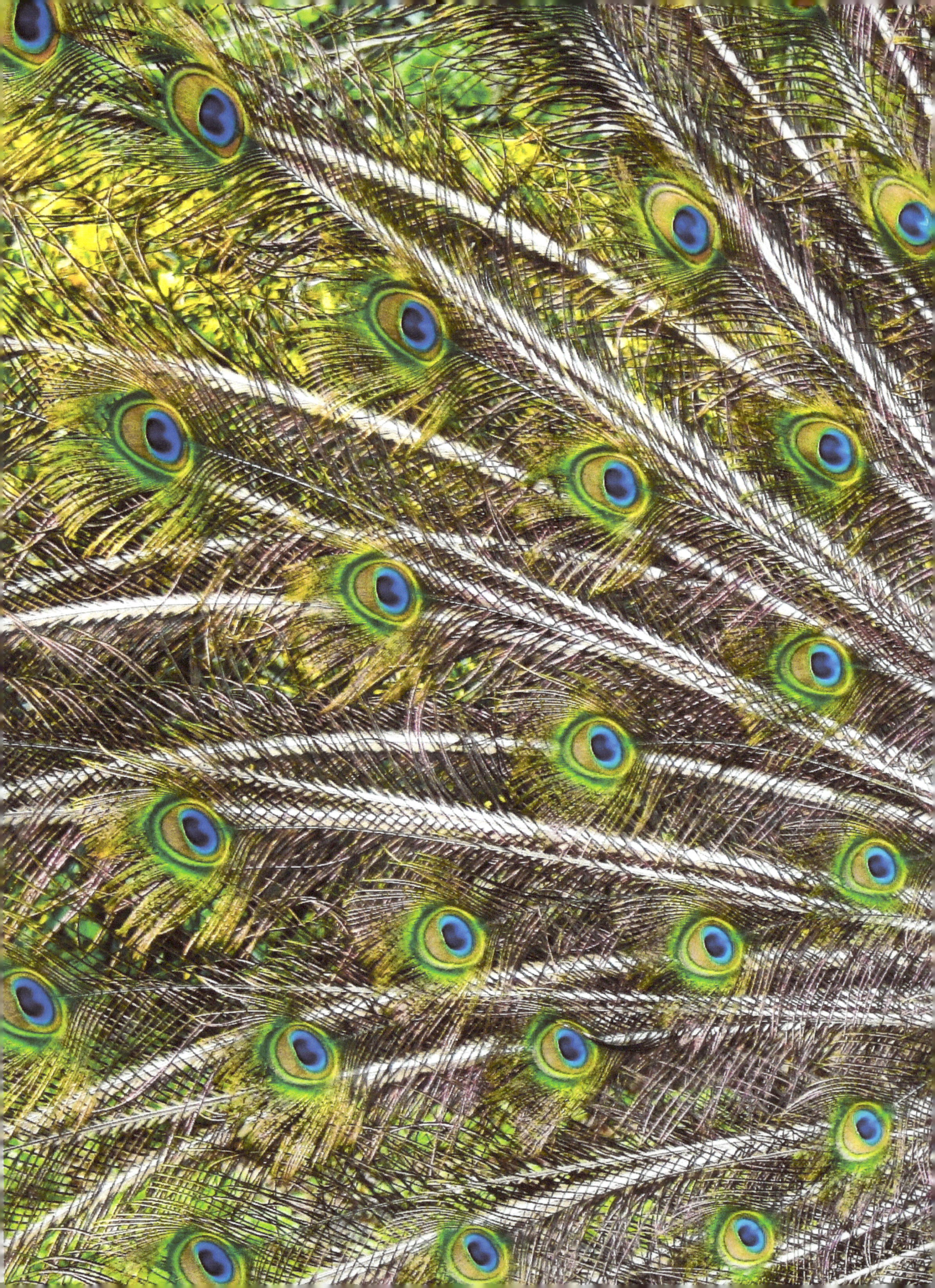

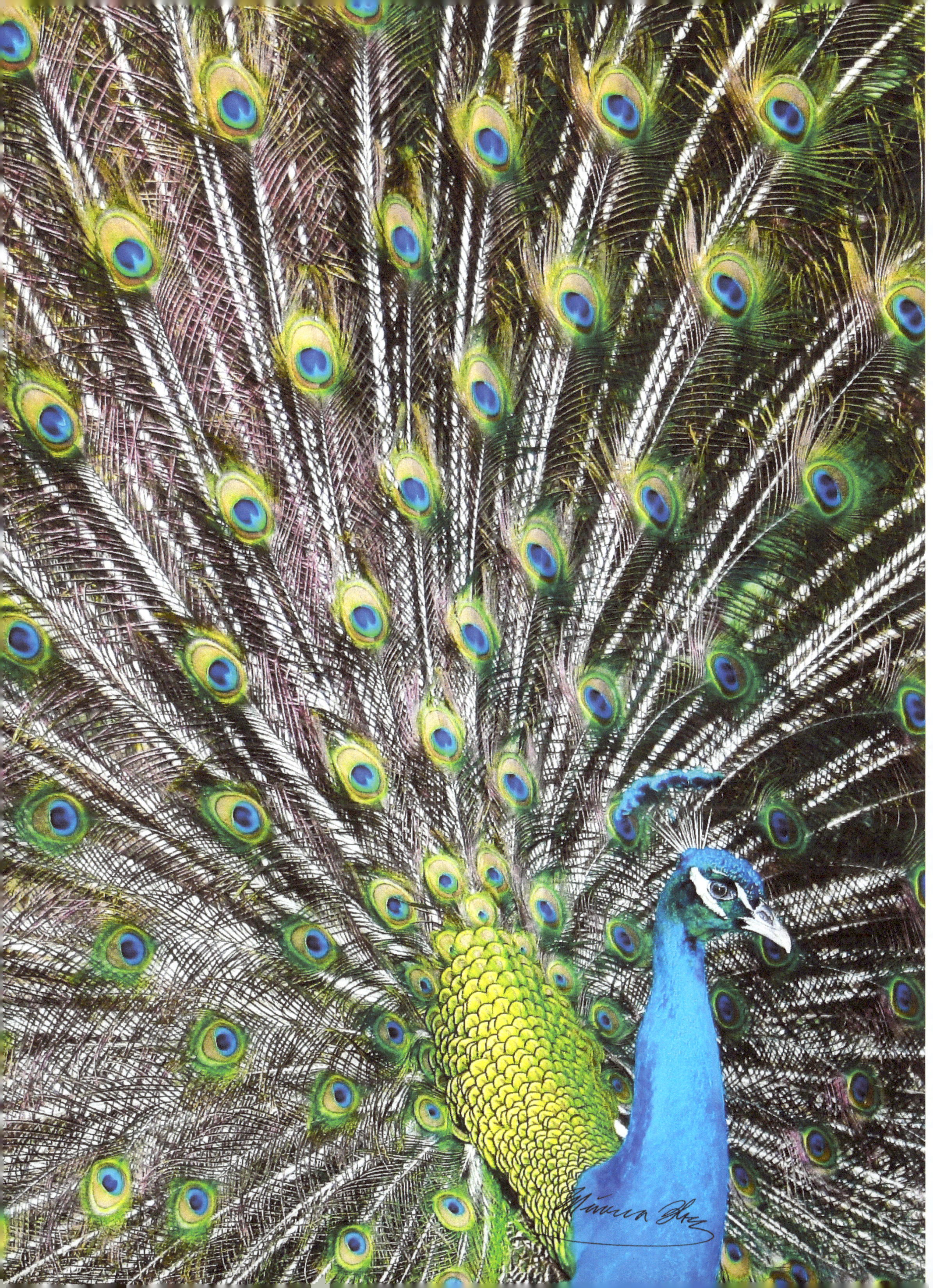

Markos Berndt

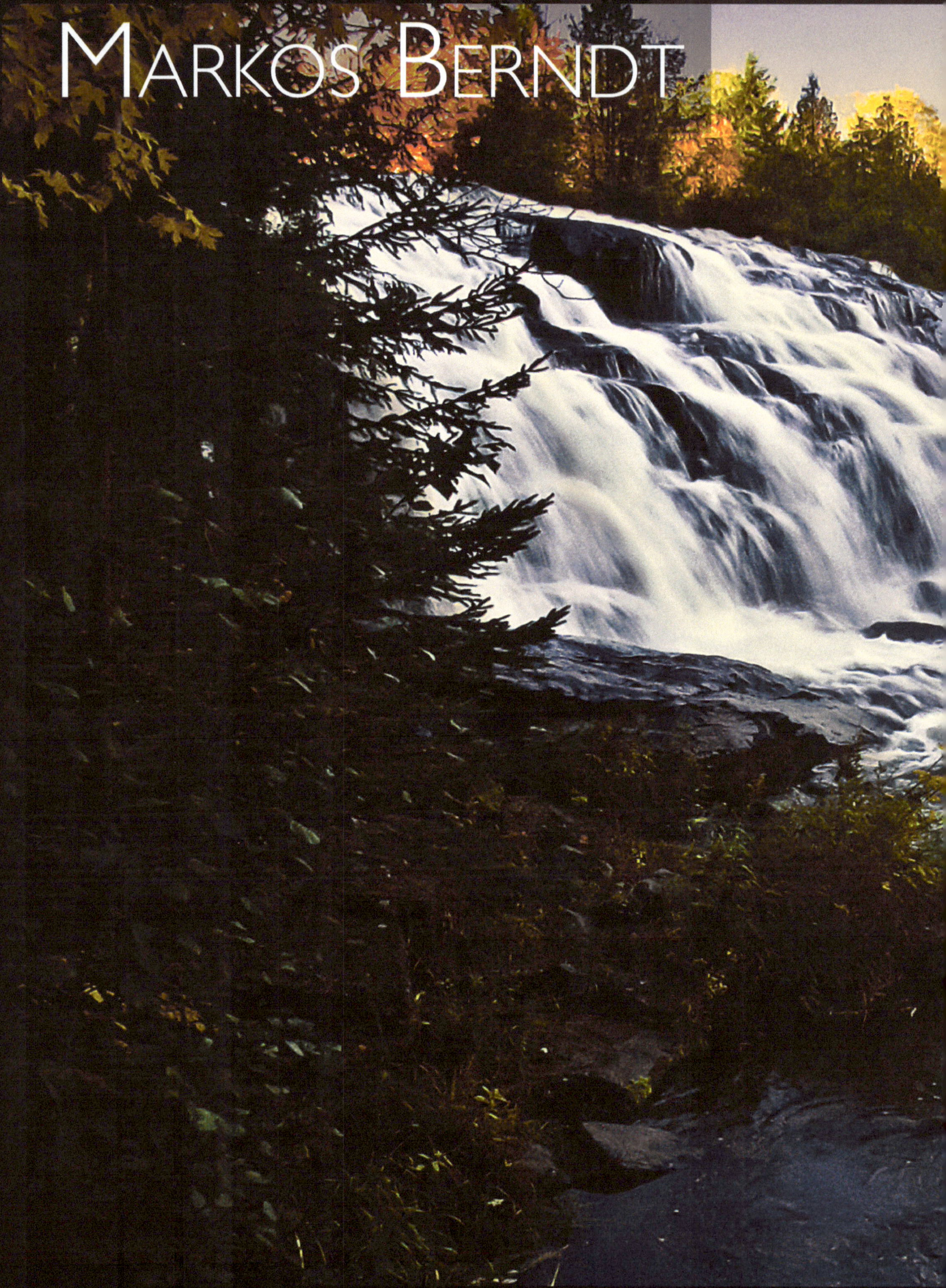

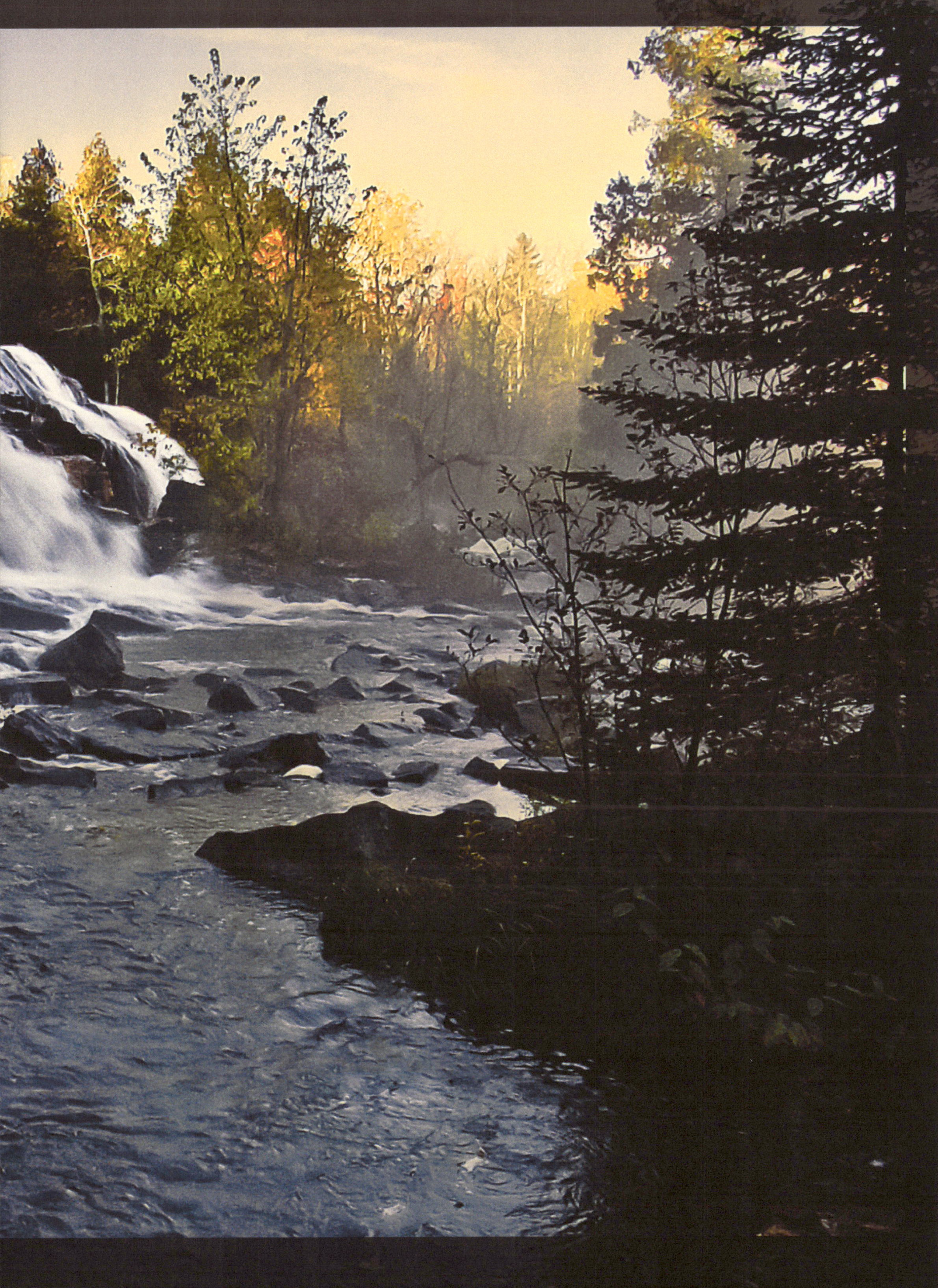

As a river runs, traversing land, intersecting larger bodies of water, carving sandstone and other hard rocks over time, it never stands still. Like life, it has a beginning and an end, only to be returned to where it once began, to start the process once more. Water gives life and in some events takes it. Without it we don't exist, at least not in our current form.

Using this medium, I hope to fully explain why I find water to be so very important in my photography, even in the places it doesn't seem to exist. I will start out with white water, mainly waterfalls, and then move onto the sandstone arches in Utah's very famous Arches National Park, and onto my favorite subject: Lake Michigan in winter.

I've been taking pictures for nearly 10 years. When I first started out, the majority of my images revolved around flowers. I would photograph them in every possible way, indoors, outdoors, with lamps and lights, setup on tables, in vases, everything. Rarely going outside that comfort zone. I found that taking steps away from what was comfortable made me a little better.

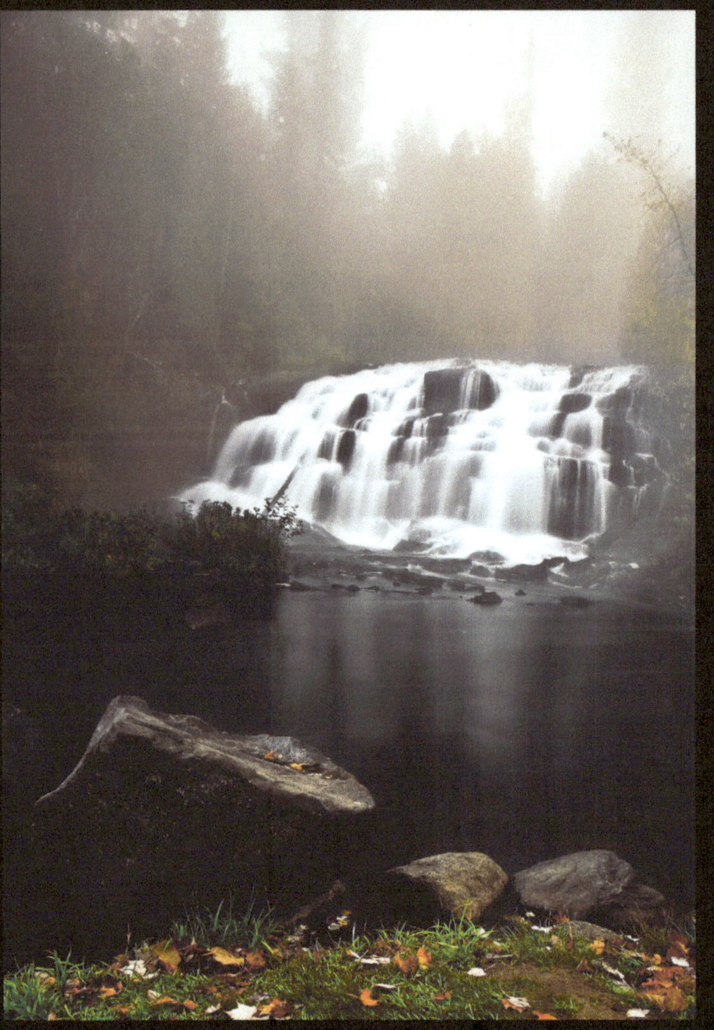

My first foray outside this comfort zone started with someone else's image of a waterfall. I wanted badly to learn how to make the water look smooth. When you're new to photography, the smallest of things are so interesting and you see the world so differently. Back then, an online photo group I participated in was filled with people who knew how to make the water smooth (I found later the technique is called veiling). I asked, but no one answered. Lucky for me, I'm persistent. Eventually, a fellow member and now I can call him a friend, Brad Fusco, responded to my annoying question.

Brad came through, and listed the things I needed (camera capable of 1/4 - 1/2 second exposure, ND filters, tripod, and shutter release and a waterfall or white water river or stream). Seems pretty straightforward equipment as I had the camera and a $25 dollar tripod, but that was it. Making my way to bhphoto.com I bought the rest, except the waterfall, those are difficult to order.

Walking around as I always did, I made my way to a small lake contained by a levee and for all intensive purposes, I will call it a waterfall, as I have since named it Whitnall Falls, which is located within Whitnall Park in Hales Corners, Wisconsin. You can see an image of "Whitnall Falls" on page 57.

My first attempts were admirable, as I looked at the images on my 1" LCD on the back of the camera. They looked OK on the monitor at home as well. Still, I wasn't getting the same feeling as I did with the first veiling image I saw. Was I doing something wrong?

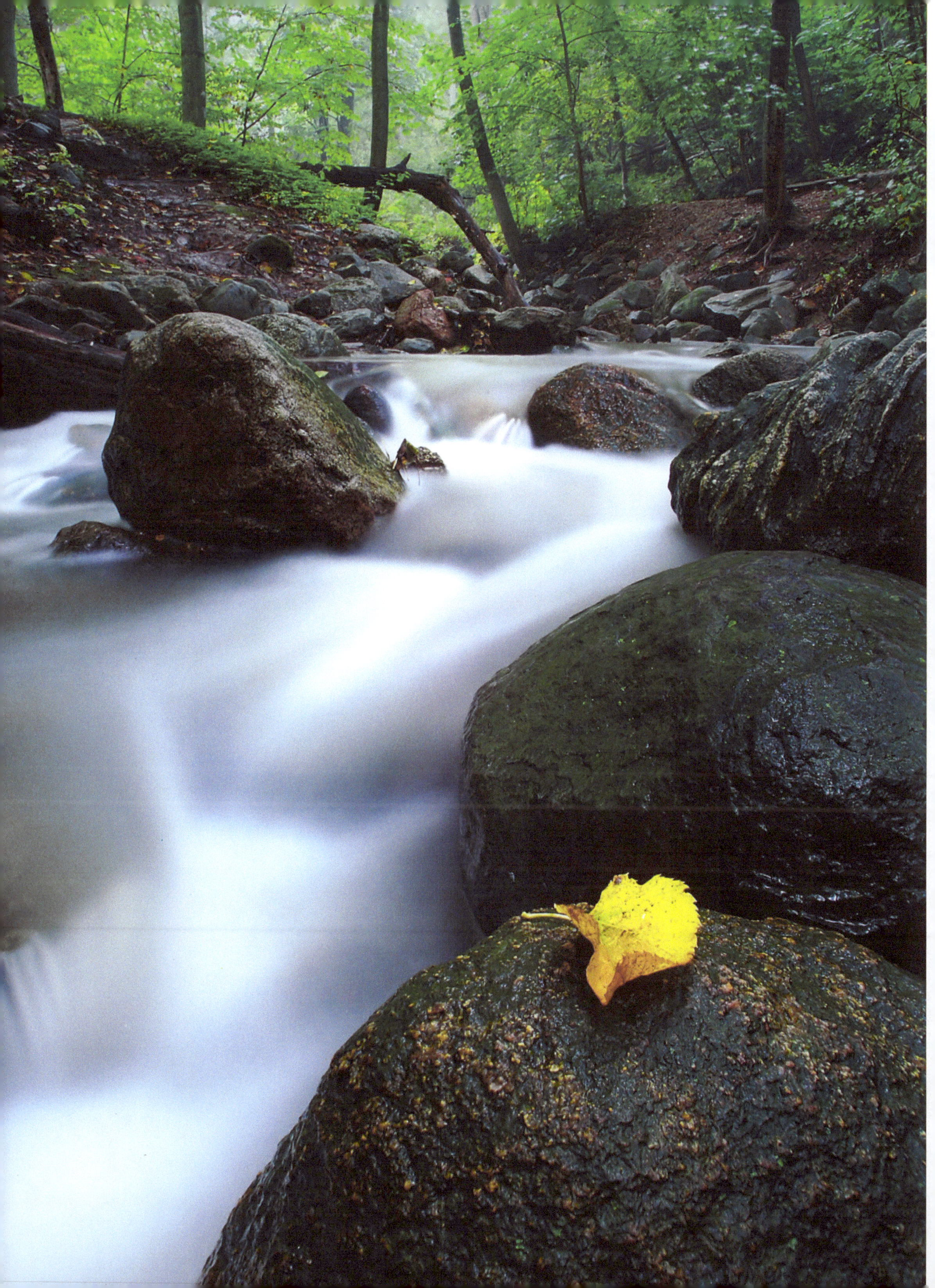

It turns out I needed a longer shutter speed to accomplish a smoother veil: less water = longer exposure. My camera at the time could only handle up to 30 seconds, and it was a very noisy image at 30 seconds. I decided to find another water source to try out. I made my way down to Lake Michigan and found a walkway that leads to the lake which contains a river, well more like a stream.

The next time it rained I would be there, so one morning, I decided it was best to make my way down to a dark location. I found a nice area to shoot from, as the trees above me were brighter than the foreground, so I took some practice shots. I reviewed them, and they seemed nice . The 30 second exposure was much better and the water looked like a wave wrapping around the rock. All the water images I photograph, land somewhere in the range of 5-30 seconds as I have found that range works best for me.

My thing at the time and I guess to this day, is to present the image with a medium-to-strong foreground or to include an element to make the scene stronger. For this purpose, I found a yellow leaf and placed it on a rock and took a few more shots. Some may say it's wrong, but I'll argue, as that leaf or any other leaf could have easily landed there. You can see the final image from that shoot on page 53. The image is called "River Runs". Some have criticized me for this approach, but over the years I 've become good at ignoring those who think its wrong, or say it doesn't look natural . Last time I checked, photography can be classified as art . I have chosen to shoot as art and to fulfill what my mind and eyes see, which ironically is normally better than the scene actually looks. Ok enough preaching. I like moving water so much that a friend and I went to Smoky Mountain National Park. It's loaded with white rivers and waterfalls. I don't have the space to put many images, so I used one that is located on page 56. You can see the water's smoothness due to a longer exposure. I was fortunate that very little wind occurred in that shot to be noticed.

The best thing about water is no matter how many times you photograph a location you will always come up with a different look. For example, let's take Whitnall Falls: you can setup a tripod and begin taking shots and one image will look different, even at the same shutter speed.

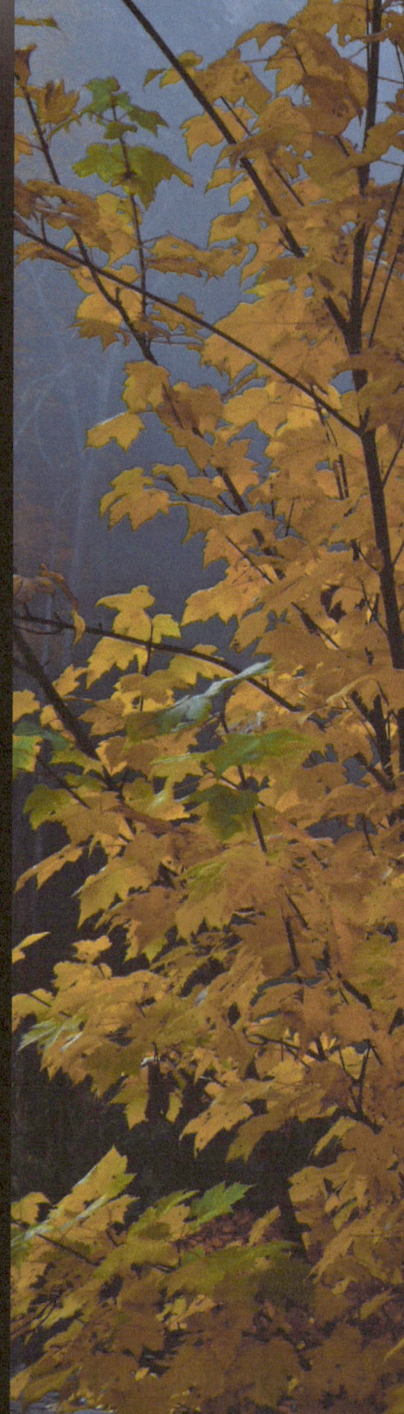

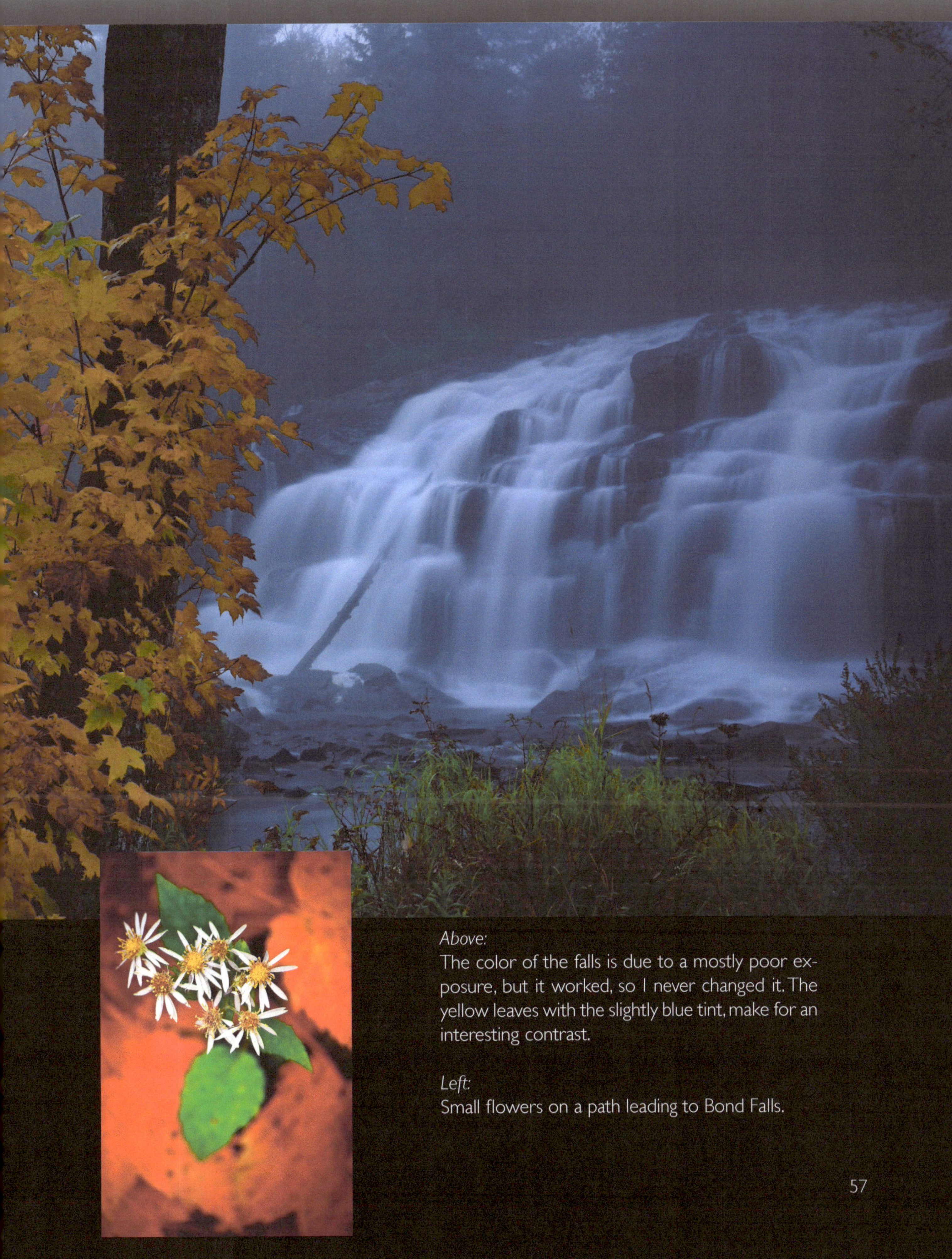

Above:
The color of the falls is due to a mostly poor exposure, but it worked, so I never changed it. The yellow leaves with the slightly blue tint, make for an interesting contrast.

Left:
Small flowers on a path leading to Bond Falls.

Water is never consistent in the way it falls, you could stare for 10 minutes and trick yourself into finding a rhythm, but as soon as you start photographing, the pattern is never the same. I was craving a real waterfall to photograph, so I did some research for waterfalls in northern Wisconsin. I was able to find a rather big one in a map book I had of Upper Michigan. I traveled with a friend and we ended up at Bond Falls.

It's the loudest and biggest waterfall I have ever seen. I liked it so much, that I try making it up there every year in early Fall, to capture the colors and the mist coming off the falls. My other images of waterfalls are of Bond Falls. It's impressive in size and in loudness and it's held back by a dam— which often makes me wonder if that's the best way to control nature.

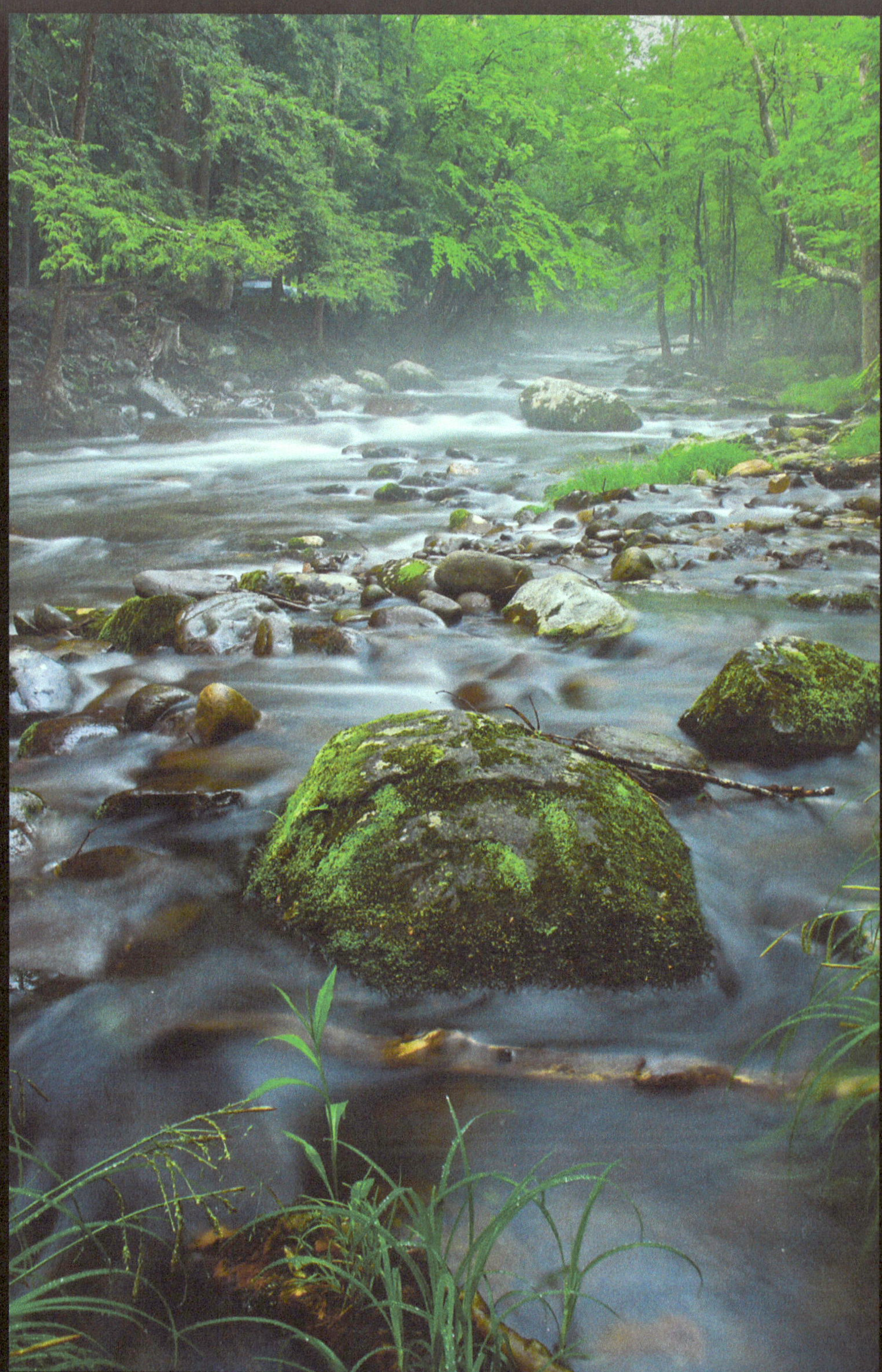

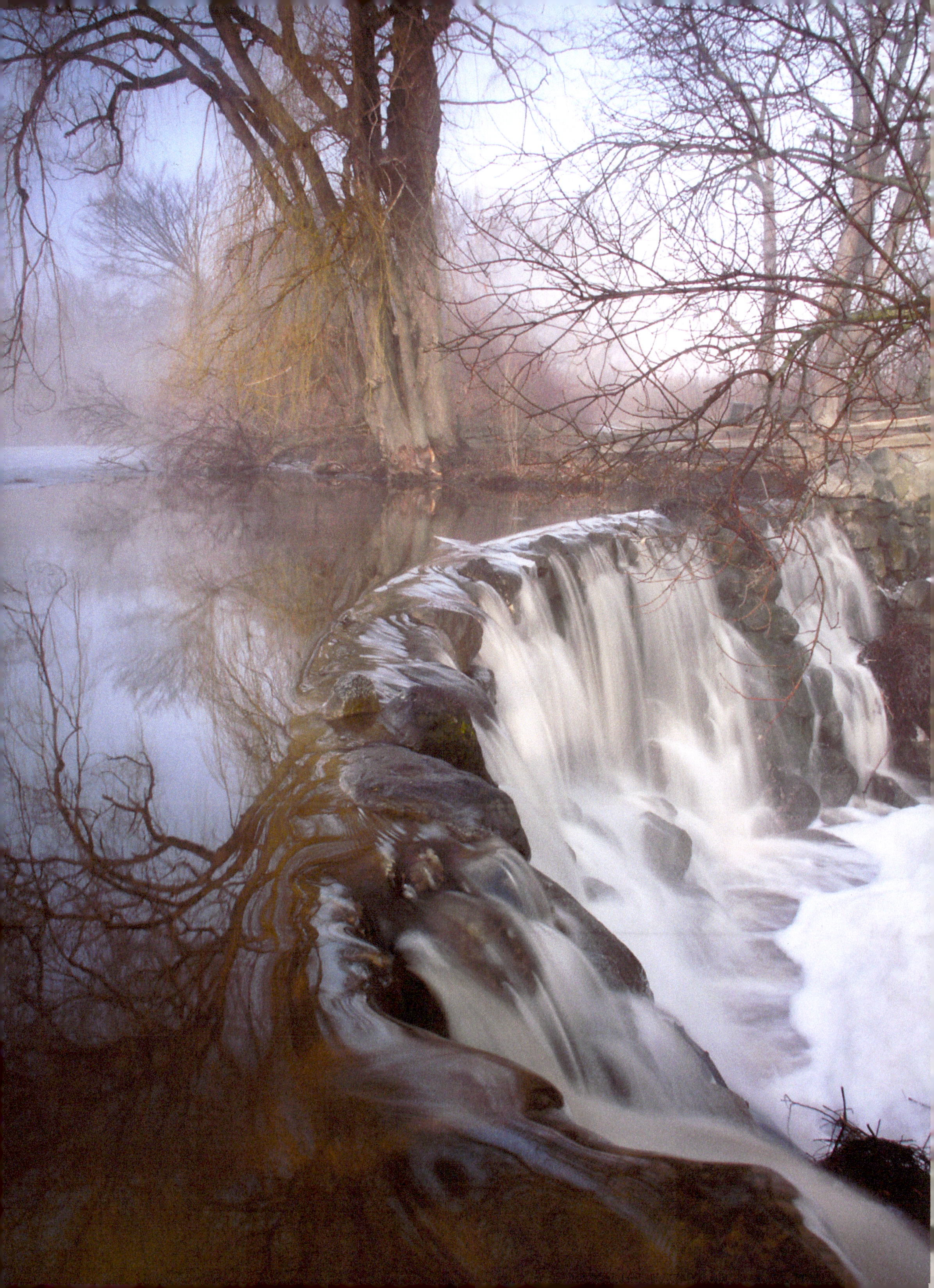

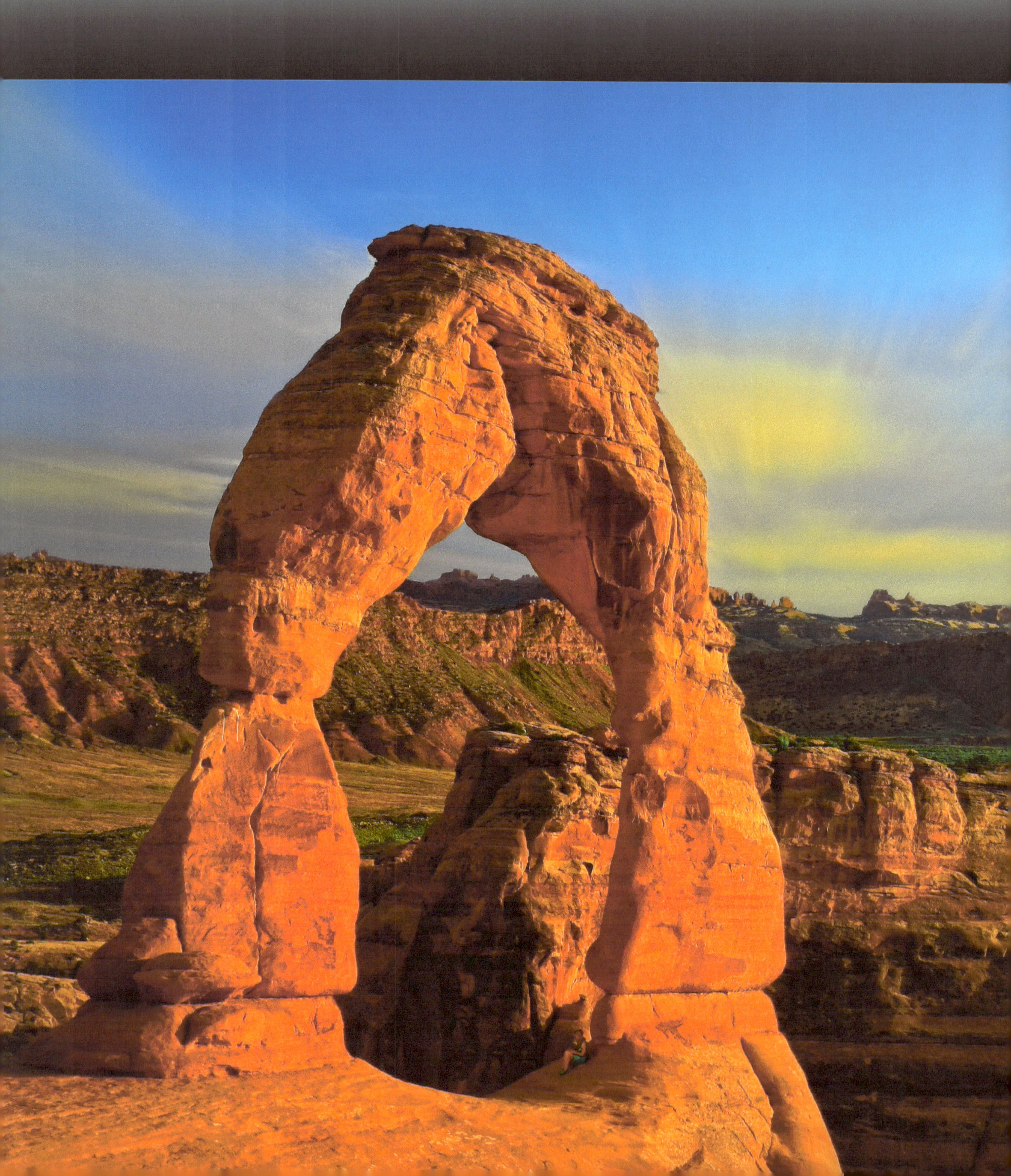

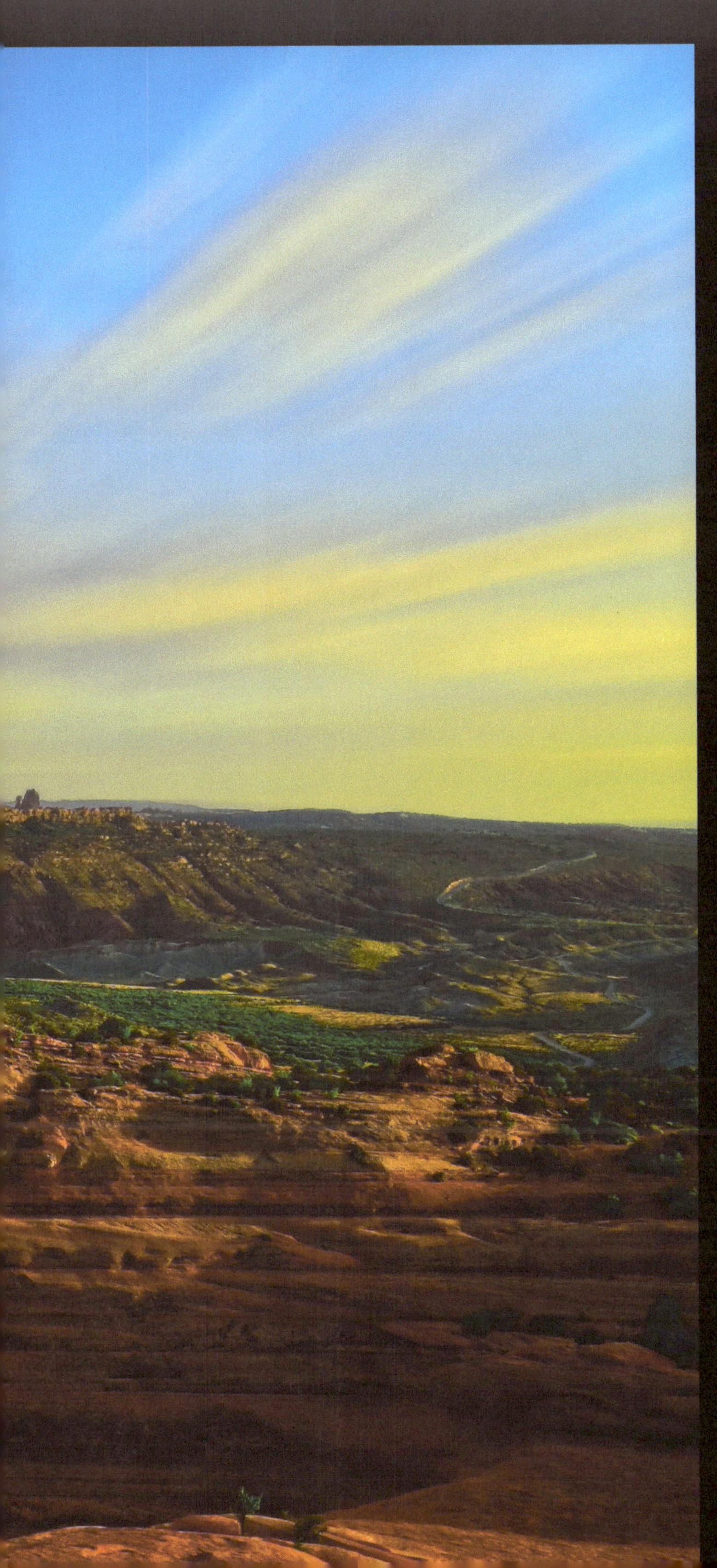

Arches National Park in Utah is the last place you might associate with water. Being a desert, you think: lack of water. It does rain and snow in Moab, which is where the park is located. It's this rain that brings life and also slowly carves away at the sandstone structures within the park. According to the park's Visitor Center, the area was once under water many billions of years ago.

I have been to Utah three times, each time visiting Arches. It's by a long shot my favorite location to photograph and actually my favorite place to hike, climb and just have fun. You can spend a week in the park and barely see everything. It has many hiking trails and countless arches for which the park is named after.

It's a short drive to Canyonlands National Park, a mini Grand Canyon of sorts and also a place to lose a few hours or so admiring the panoramic vistas.

Admiring images from great photographers is what set me off to the West originally. Namely, Tom Till's image with yellow Wyethia scabra in the foreground of Courthouse Tower, on the cover of Outdoor Photography, which I received a short time before going to Arches for the first time.

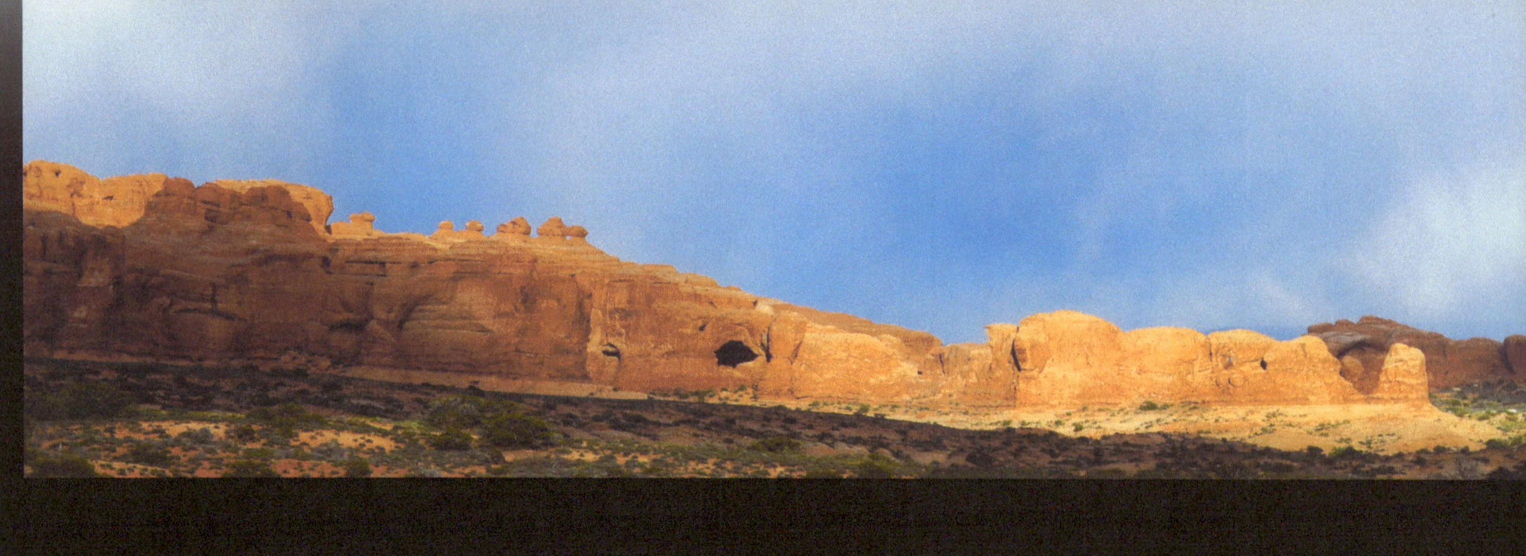

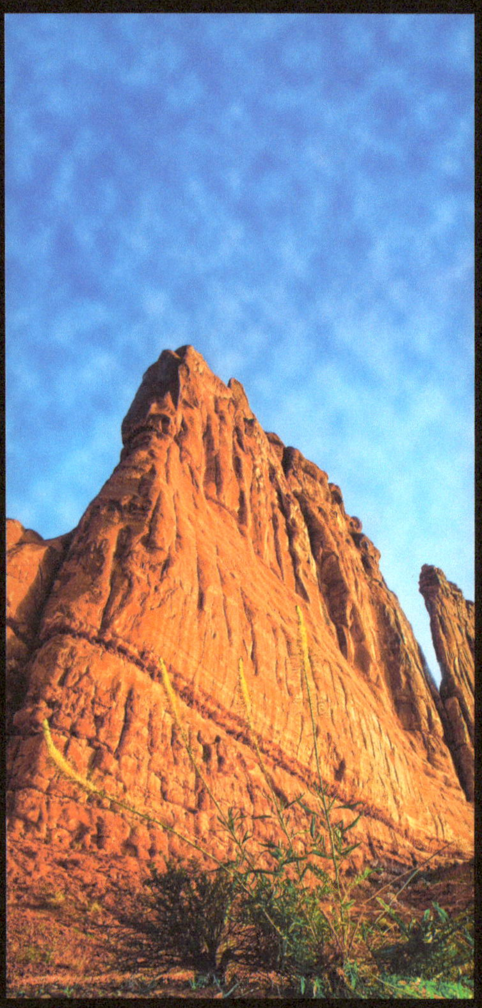

Above:
Courthouse Tower from a different perspective.

Right:
Turrett Arch as viewed from the South Window. A shot that has been done millions of times, but each will have their own story to tell on how they achieved it.

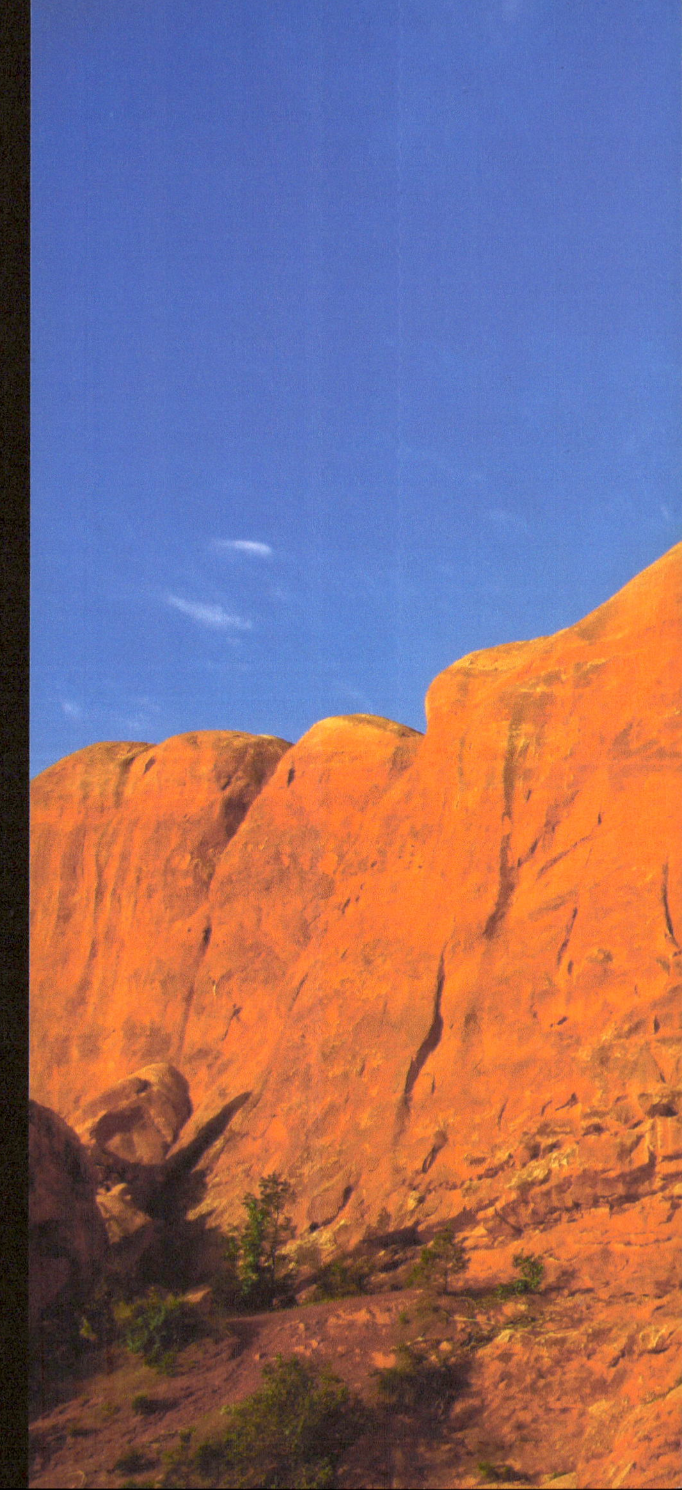

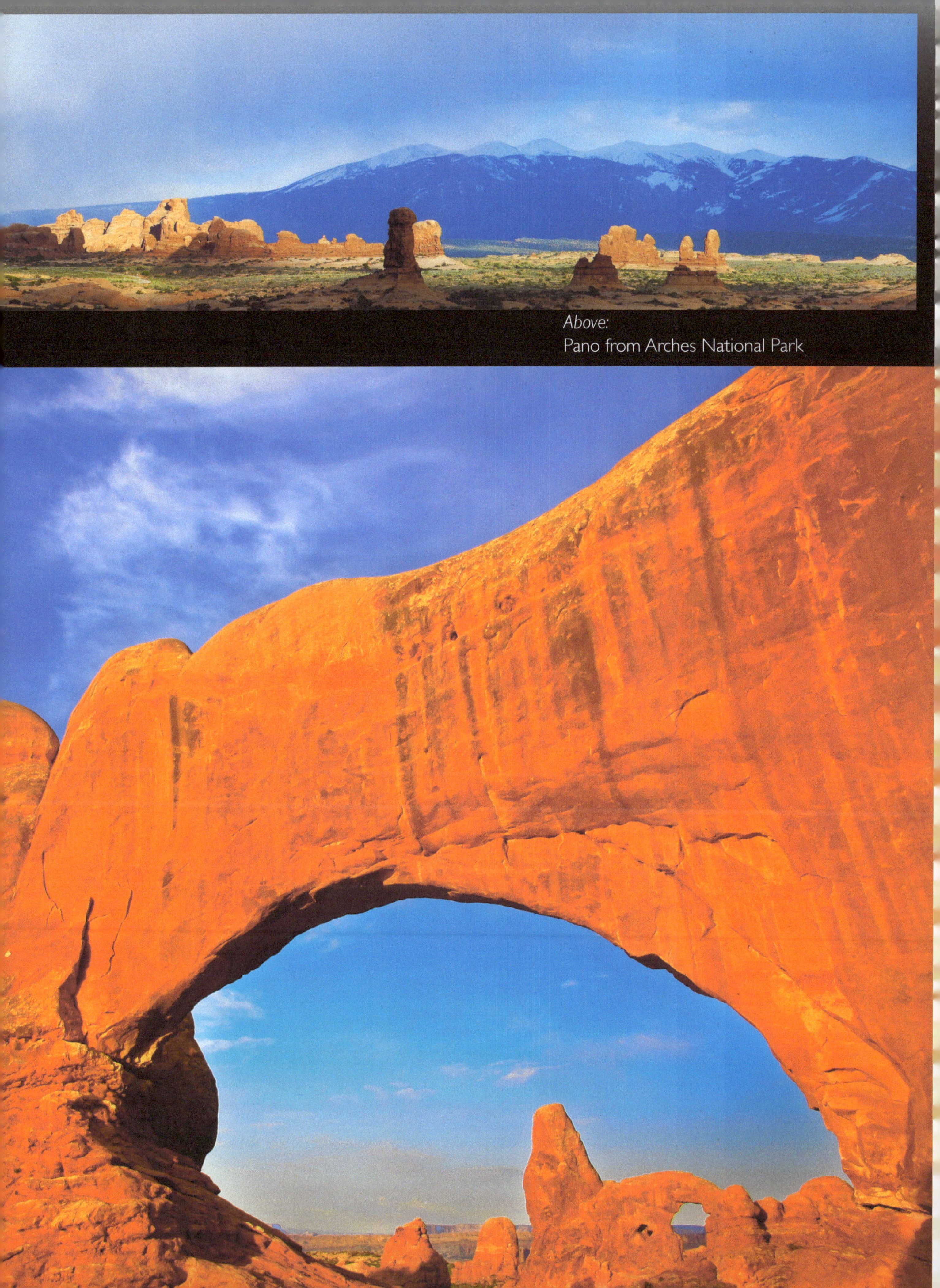

Above:
Pano from Arches National Park

When you're in the area, the one thing that stands out is the LaSal Mountains, especially when there's snow on the peeks. It makes for a beautiful contrast to the blue sky and red sandstone. My recommendation for the best time to go would be the Spring season as you will still have snow on the peeks. It recedes quickly under the hot summer sun. Fall and Winter would also be better times, less people is sometimes better.

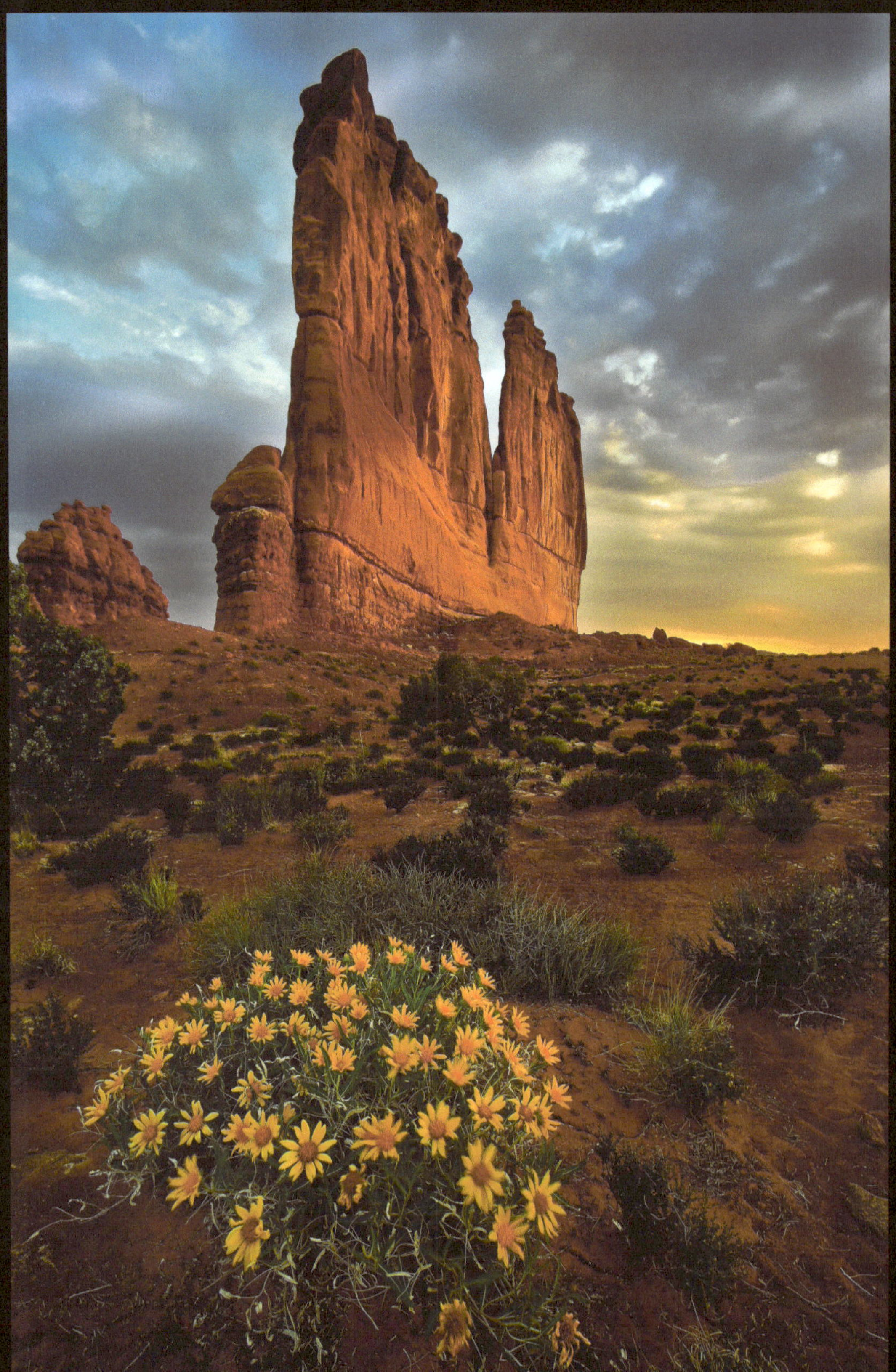

Left:
Wyethia scabra in front of Courthouse Towers. The yellow bushes are all over when I'm there in May. They make fantastic foregrounds.

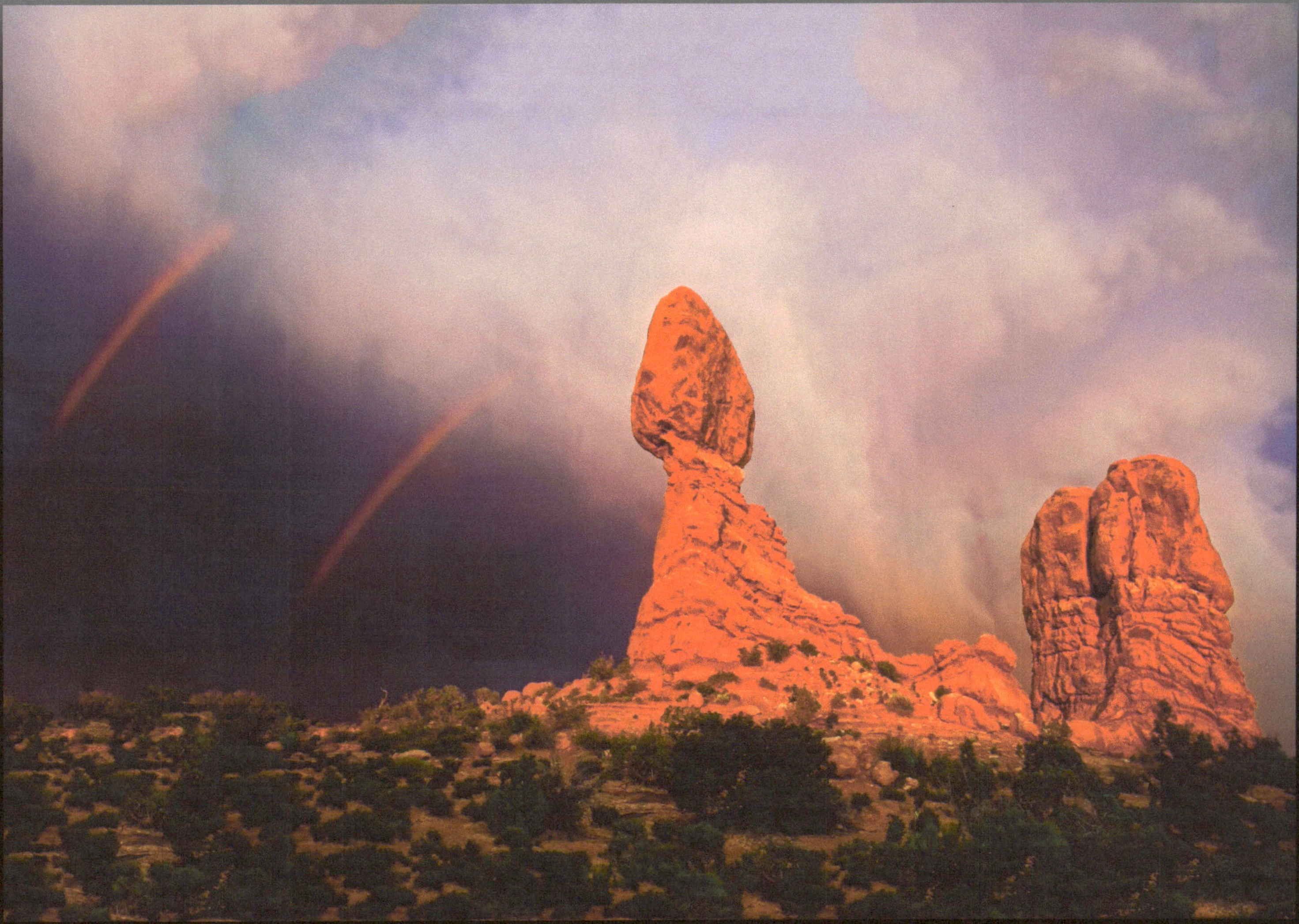

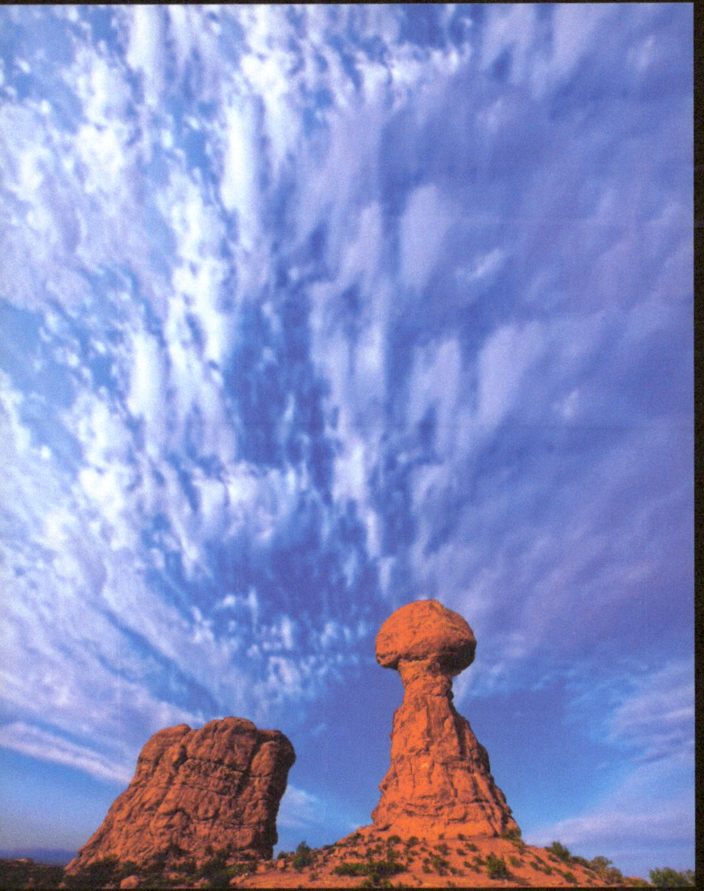

Above:

A partial double rainbow forms near Balanced Rock. It was the first time in my life the temperature dropped from near 100 F to 32 F in less than 30 Min. From my memory, driving up, I was in shorts and a tank top and I had a great feeling I would get a rainbow. Most of the people left and I told this nice German fellow to stay because something nice would happen.

Over:

Again, Balanced Rock from a different perspective. This was photographed with a fisheye lens and corrected in Photoshop to remove the distortion.

By volume, Lake Michigan is the 2nd largest of the great lakes in the United States. Choosing the winter months to photograph the lake may seem a tad odd, why should I venture out into the cold and slippery ice for a few shots?

Well, because the shoreline in winter is different than the rest of the year or at least until it snows and ice can start forming on the rocks and other objects that lay all over the shoreline. Every time I make the attempt to go down to take photos, the shore is a little different. Broken ice will drop off from surfaces and sometimes a slightly warmer weather will melt the ice formations, only to form again when the temperatures drop for a week or two.

If I'm lucky, we'll get a foot of snow and the temperature drop will harden the wave-wetted-snow. You can go from small ice shelves to something that looks as if it belongs in the Arctic but on a much smaller scale.

The emptiness of it all is what I like the most. Less people means less trash to clean up, less trash means I can concentrate on what I need to do, especially in post-processing, where I find details that I might have missed. I like to start very early. Hiking around in the dark with a flashlight looking for unique features in the ice is not exactly fun, but most people don't realize the beautiful colors happen before sunrise.

My style with water doesn't change in winter as I still prefer the low to the ground long exposures, even though my knees say NOOO! A tripod is more important when using a flashlight to paint or color the ice as the long exposure will smooth out the water.

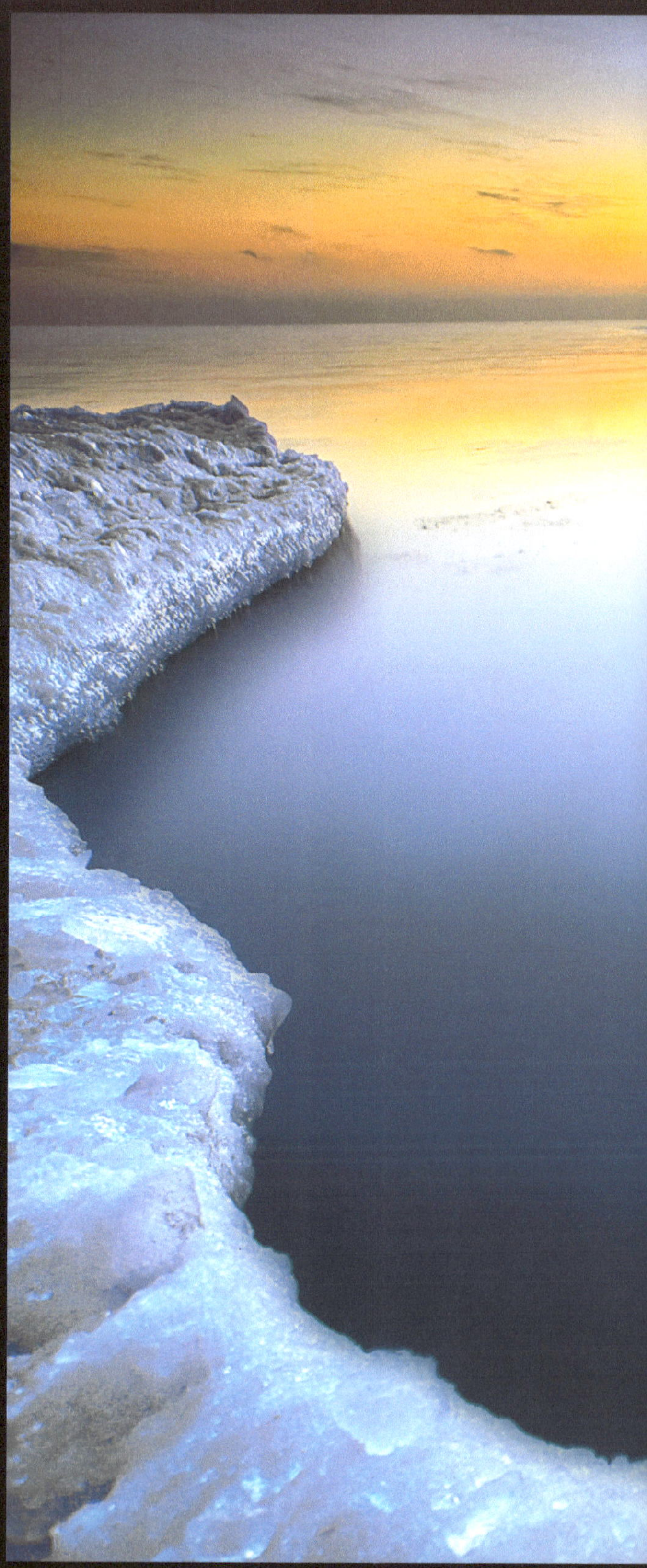

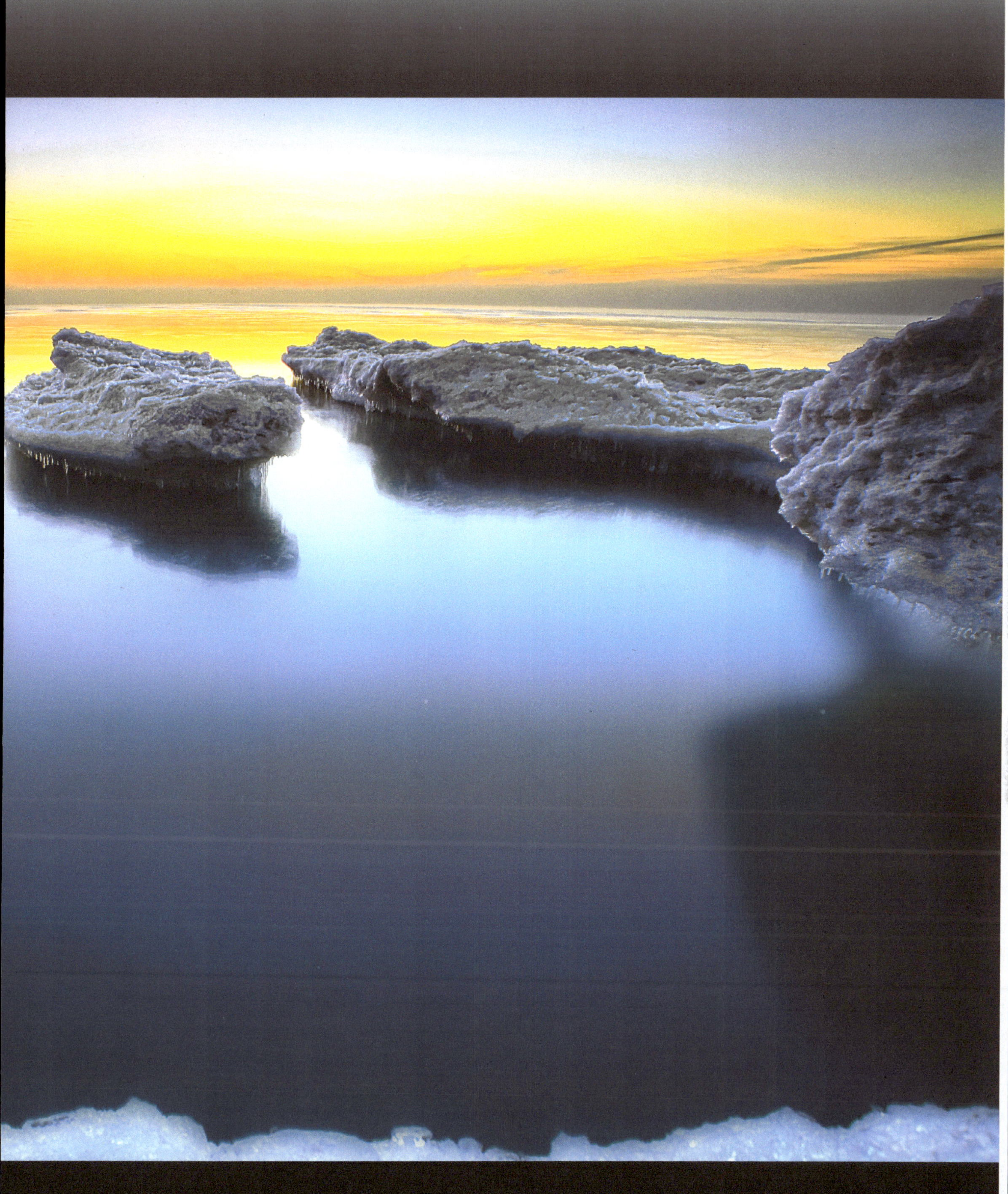

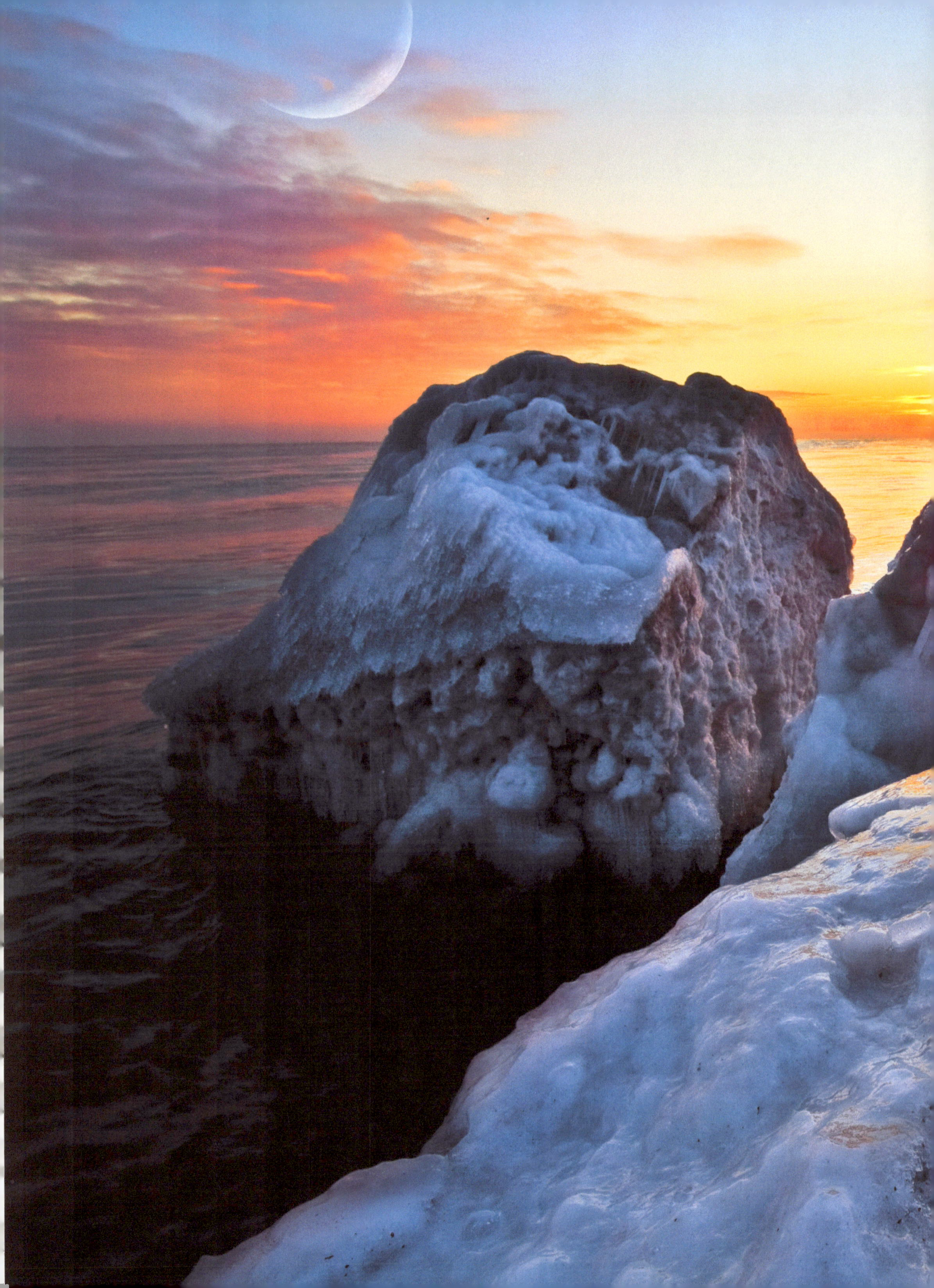

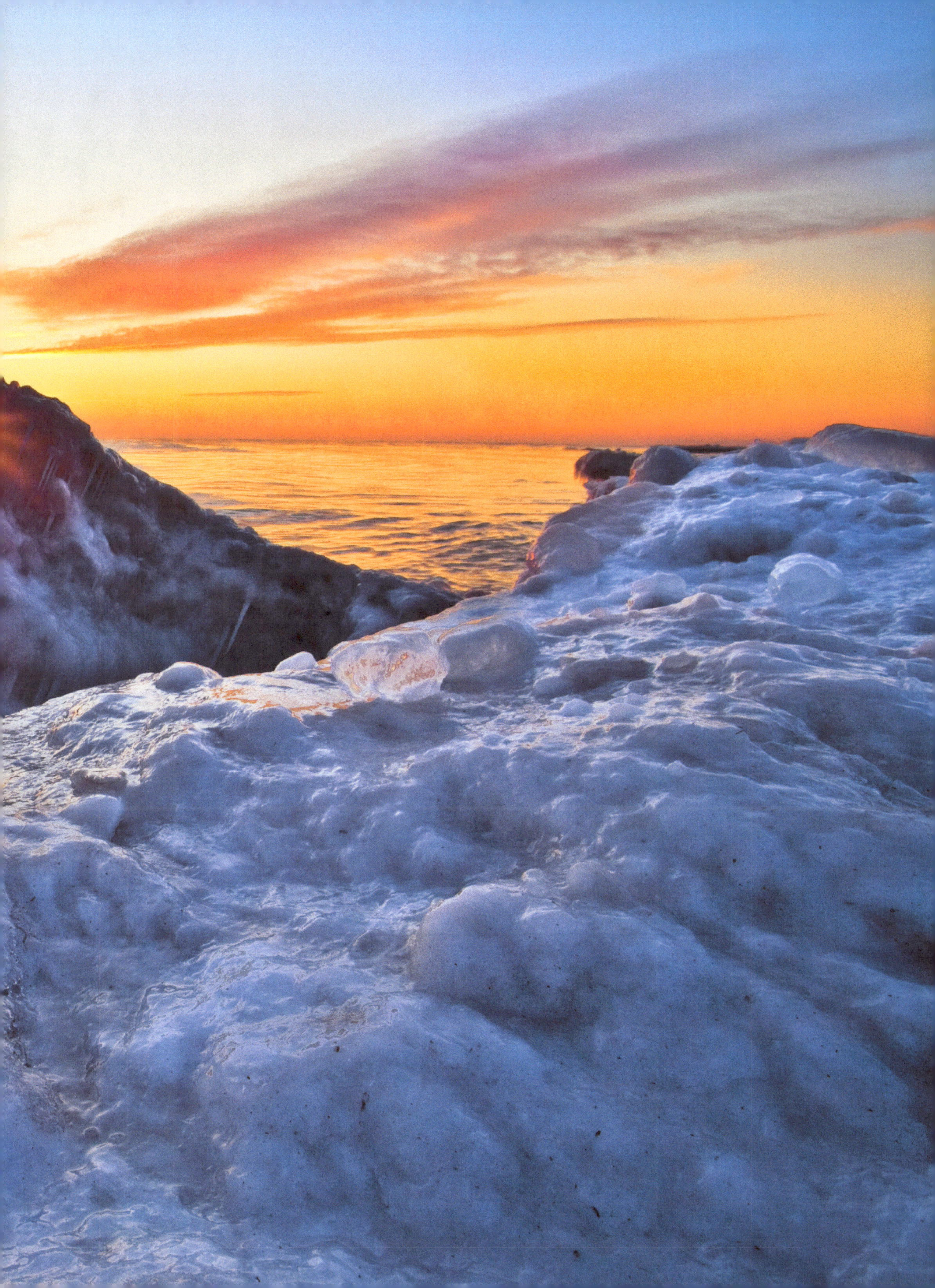

A number of winters ago it was colder than it has been. The winter of 2003 brought more floaters and even some icebergs and ice shelves along the lake's horizon. Only a few times have they been close enough to get a good photograph.

Being able to endure the cold is not as difficult as it sounds. I had to turn back once and that was due to a wave getting me a little too wet. I have endured -50 degrees in upper Wisconsin for 4 plus hours. If I stop moving, I will begin to feel my bones stiffen.

I'll never call myself a great photographer, but I challenge anyone to show me a better winter lake shore image than my best. That may sound a tad arrogant, but I'm hardly the type. I do what I do for the challenge of it, to constantly improve year to year. I will put more effort into Lake Michigan in winter than I do the whole summer, mostly because it needs more effort. If you happen to see a camera bag with no owner in site, please leave it, I'm usually a good distance away from my empty bag.

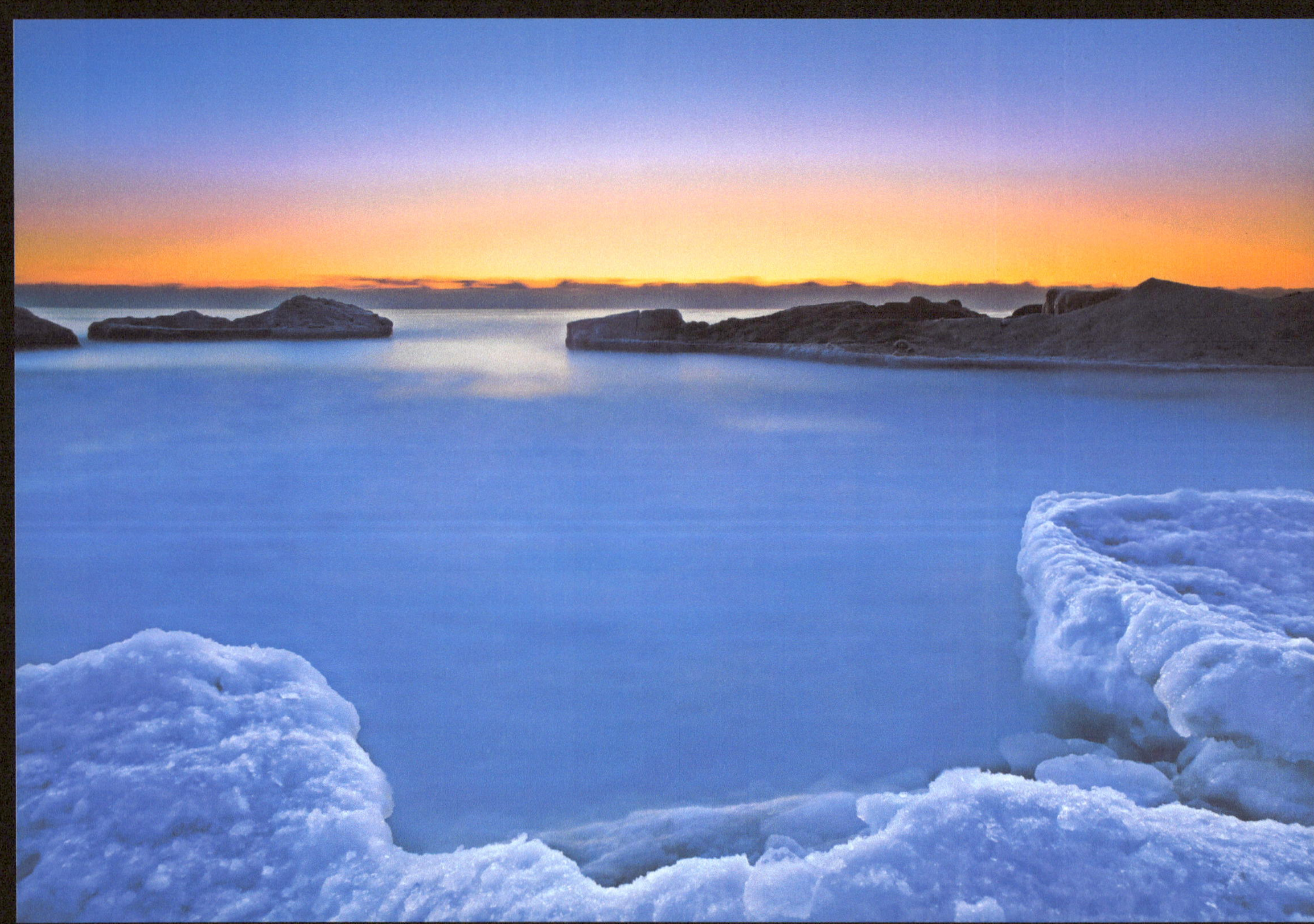

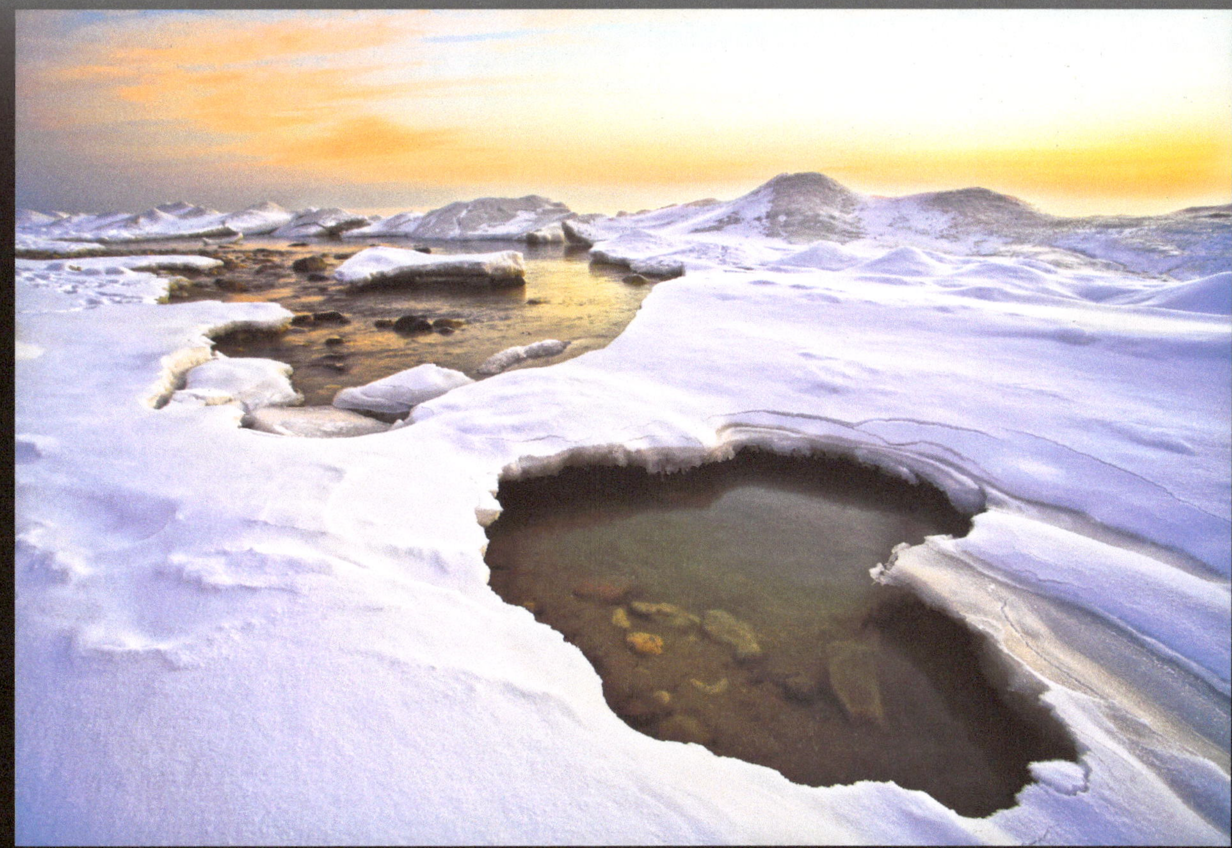

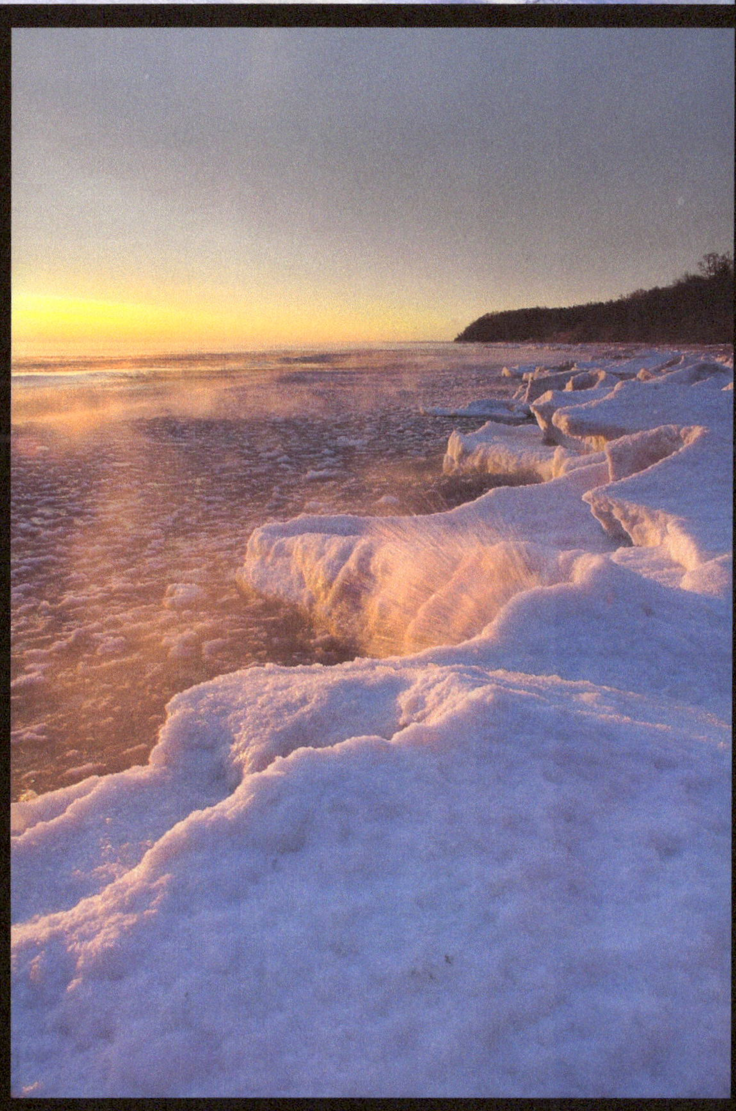

Above:
In this photo, the ice at the peeks is about 7 feet. The wide angle lens creates a surreal look to the scene. The areas where you see unfrozen water is due to the runoff coming from the cliffs and sewer to the left. I had to be more careful than normal with the soft ice and fresh snow, as it made for easy footprints.

Right:
Cold air and warm water makes for a nice sunrise in this 2003 image.

Left:
A few days after a large snowfall and below freezing weather, the accumulated snow formed a bay, in this surreal long exposure photograph.

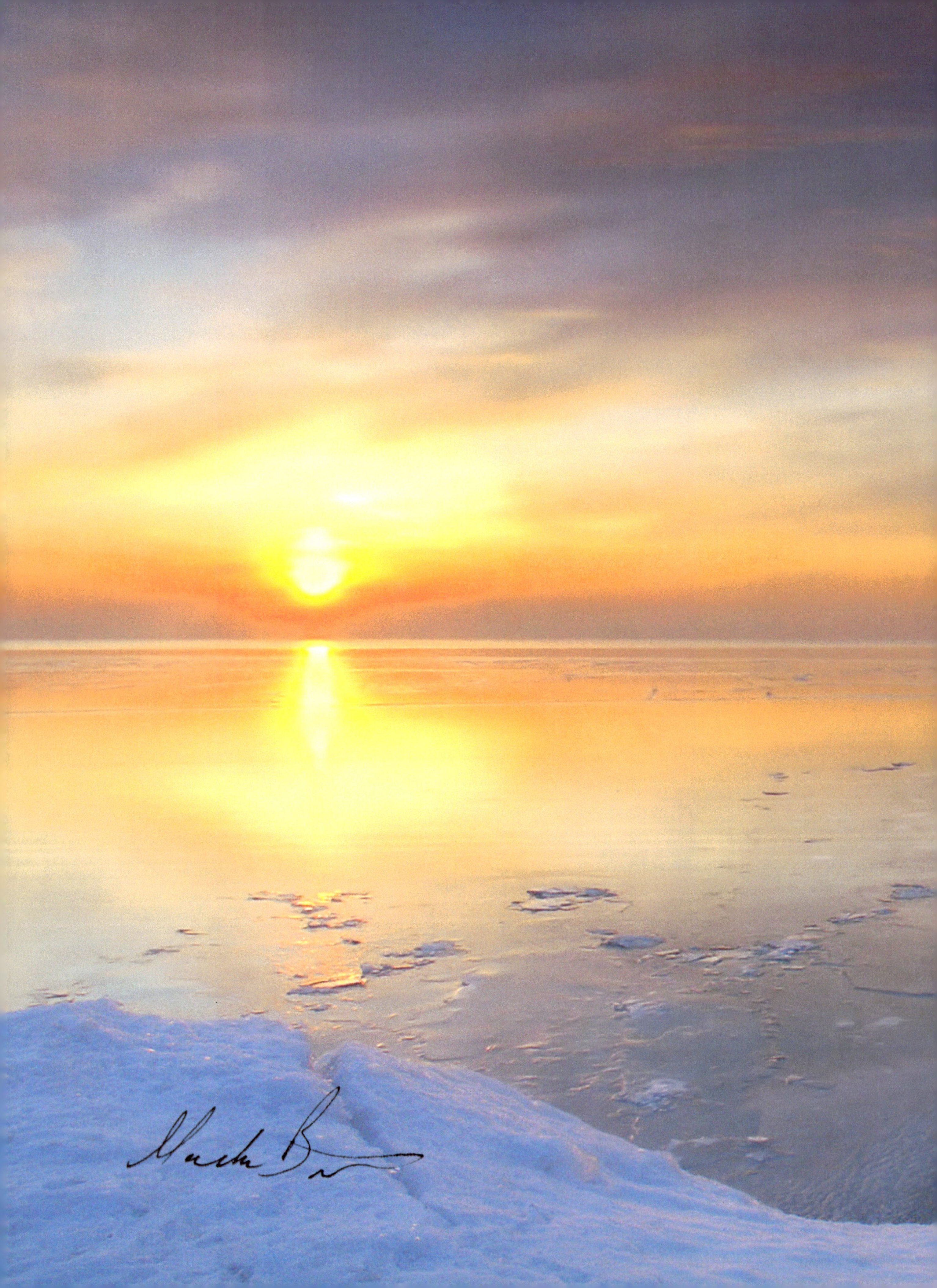

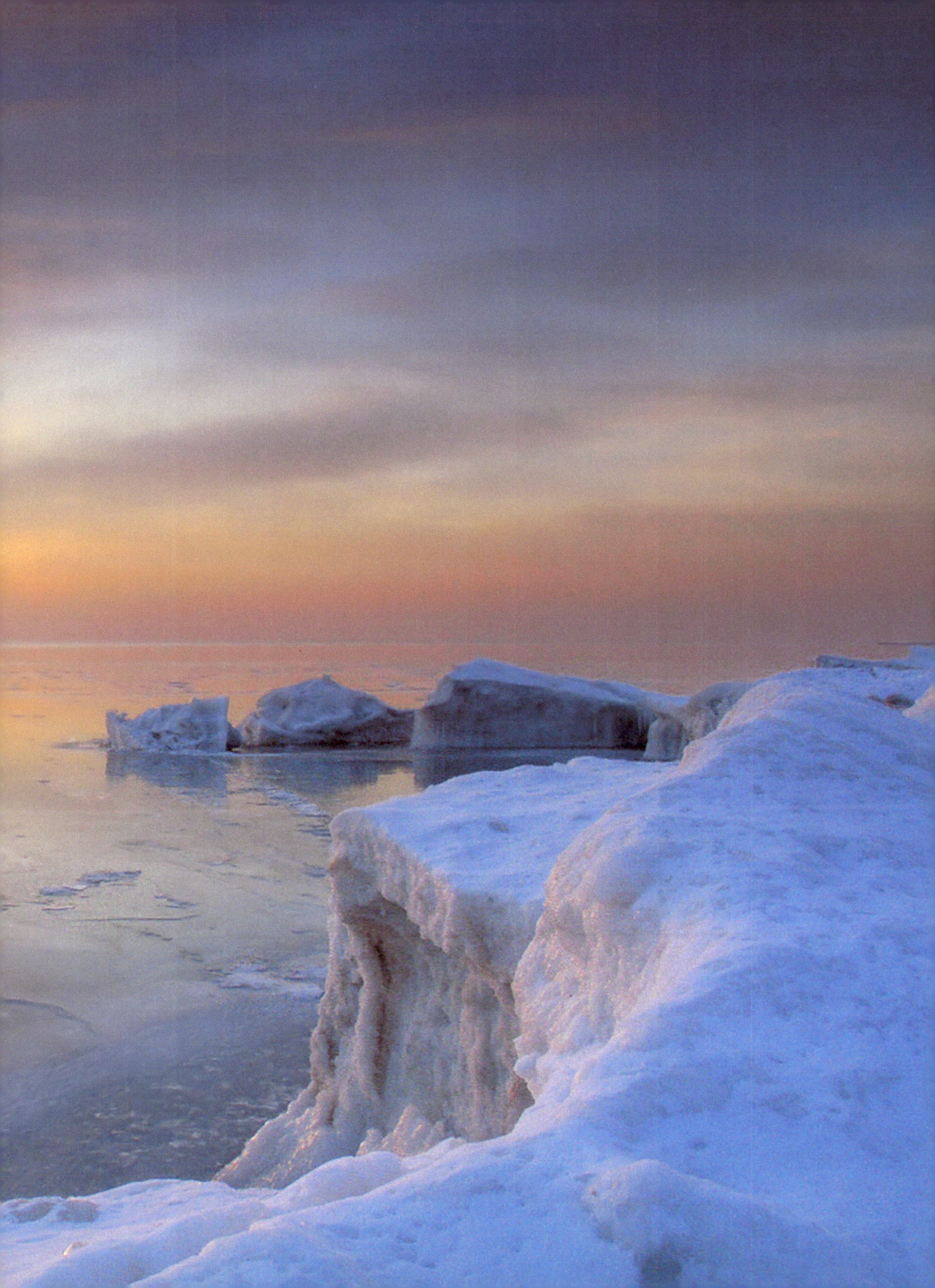

SHOOTING DATA

for select images

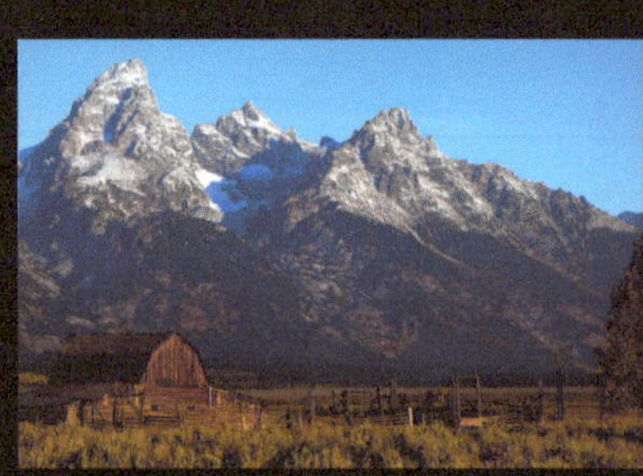

8-9

f/14 @ 1/200 sec
ISO 320

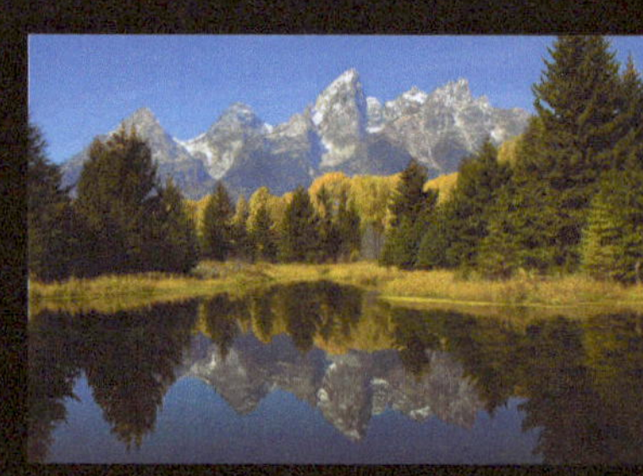

22-23

f/10 @ 1/125 sec
ISO 320

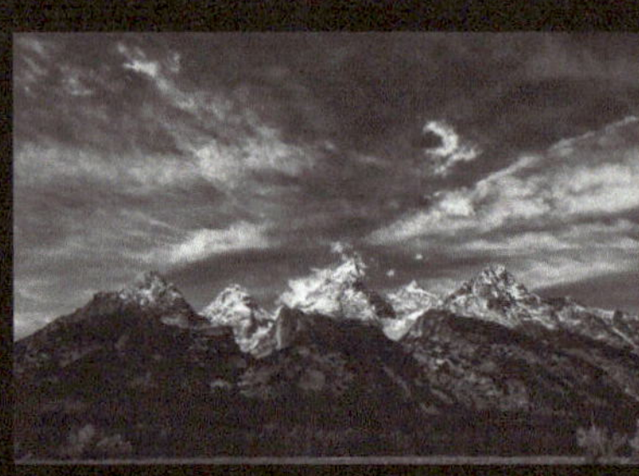

10-11

f/8 @ 1/250 sec
ISO 320

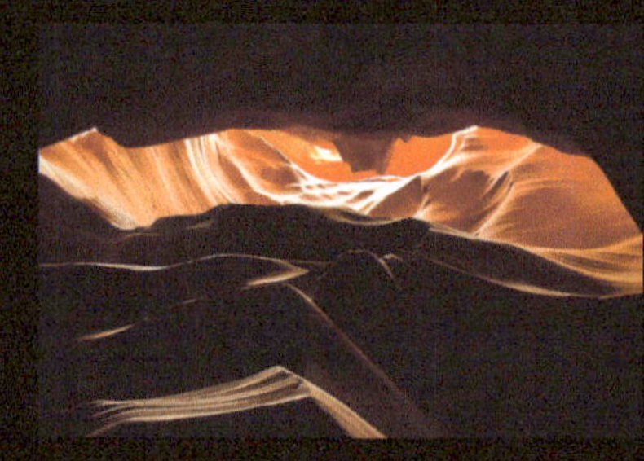

28-29

f/8 @ 1/3 sec
ISO 800
Circular polarizer

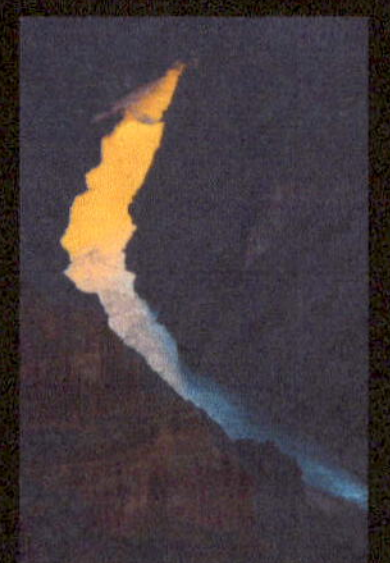

15

f/9 @ 1/40 sec
ISO 200

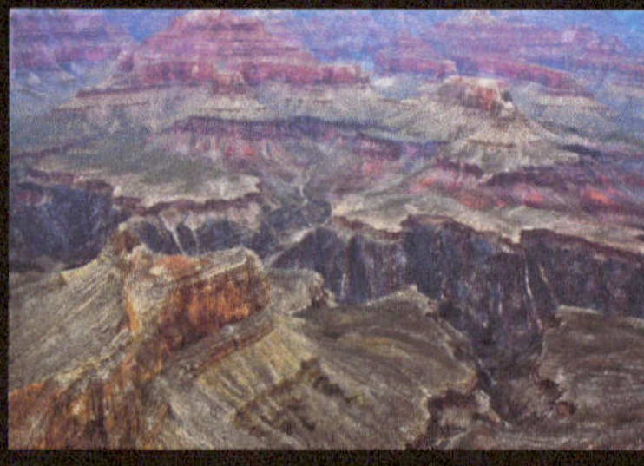

32

f/11 @ 1/45 sec
ISO 400
Circular polarizer

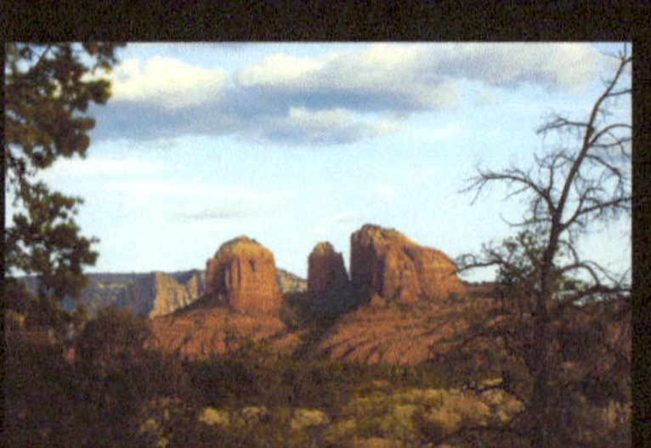

18

f/8 @ 1/125 sec
ISO 250

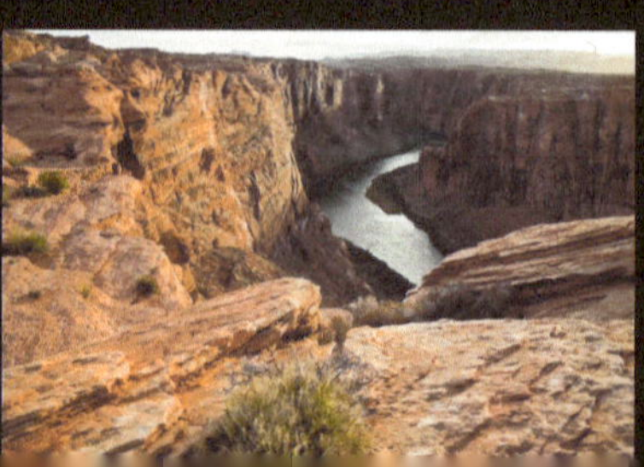

38-39

f/3.5 @ 1/125 sec
ISO 200
Circular polarizer

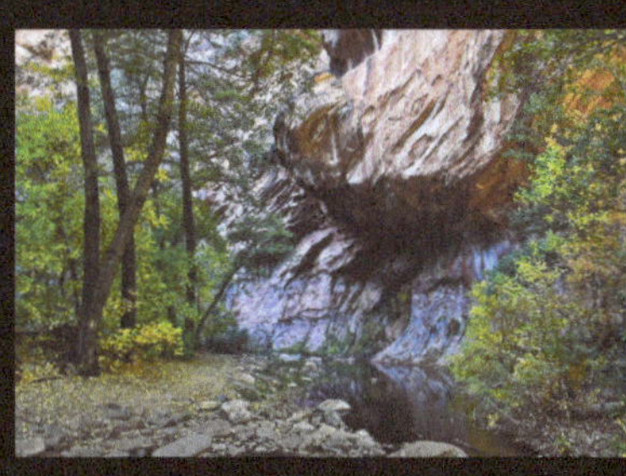

44-45

f/5.6 @ 1/30 sec
ISO 400
Circular polarizer

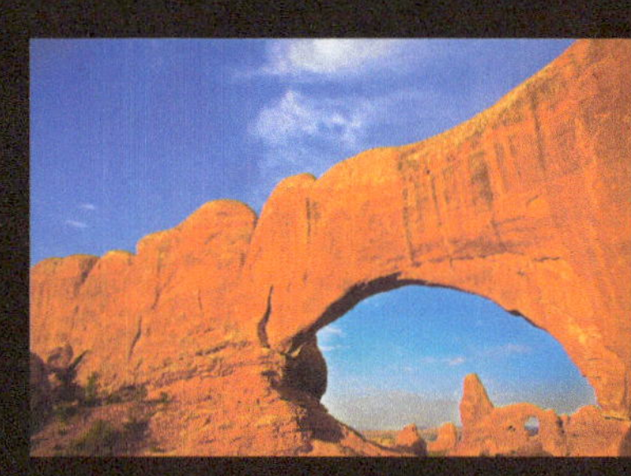

60-61

f/22 @ 1/8 sec
ISO 50

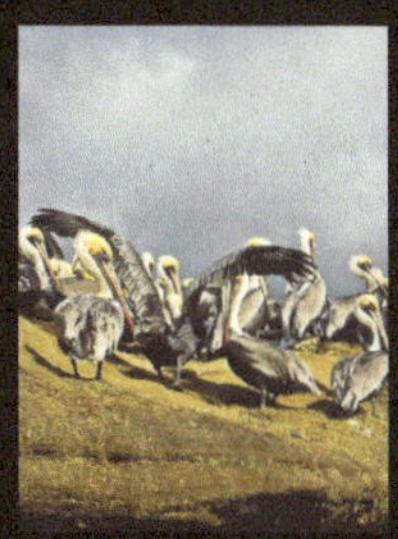

47

f/11 @ 1/200 sec
ISO 100
Circular polarizer

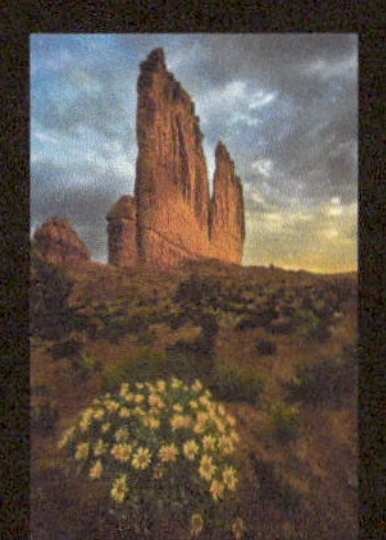

62

f/11 @ 1/4 sec
ISO 50

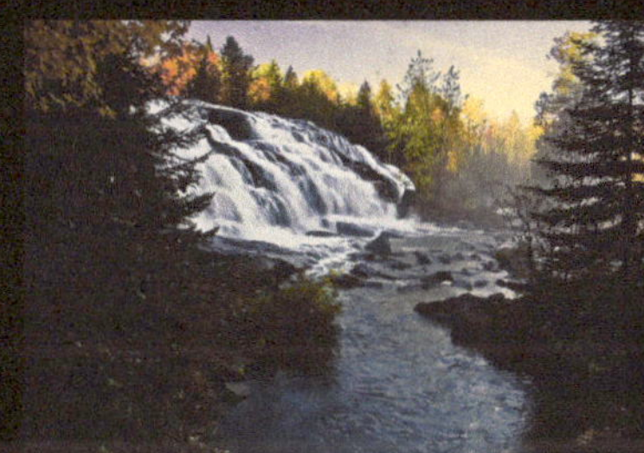

50-51

f/8 @ 1/15 sec
ISO 100
2-stop ND Grad filter

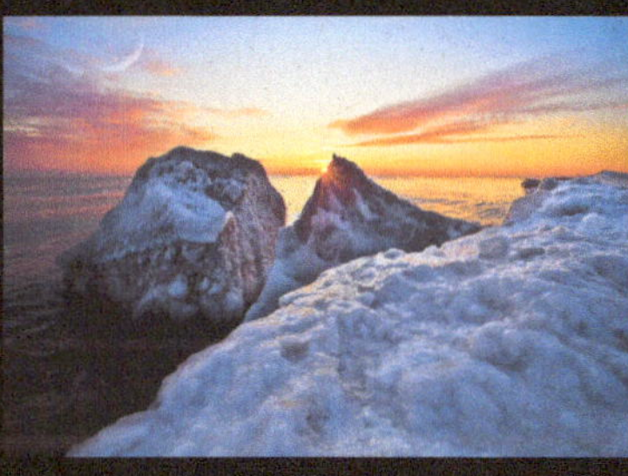

66-67

f/13 @ 1/20 sec
ISO 50
Moon added later for effect

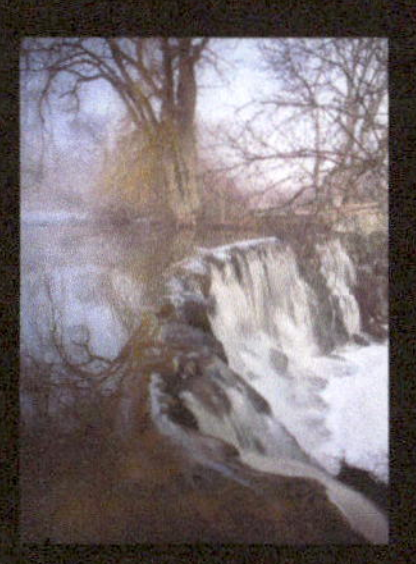

53

f/8 @ 1/3 sec
ISO 100
Circular polarizer/ 1 stop ND Grad

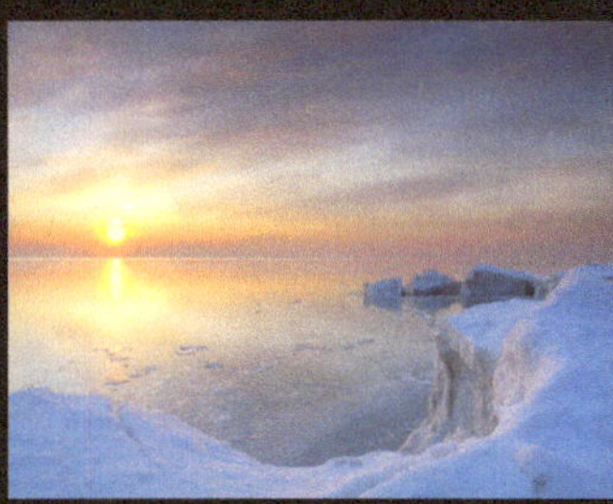

70-71

f/8 @ 1/60 sec
ISO 100
2 stop ND Grad filter

Gary Glass

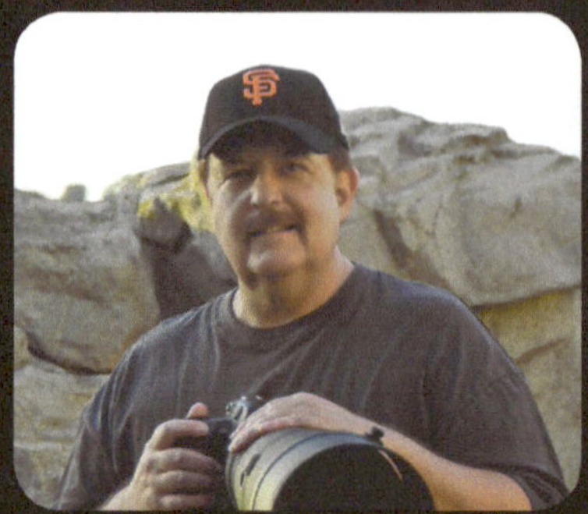

Gary is a California based Photographer who has been photographing wildlife and landscape images for 35 years. His images have been published in books and added to private and commercial collections. His images have also been used in The Yellowstone to Yukon Conservation Initiative or Y2Y a joint Canada-US charitable organization that seeks to preserve and maintain the wildlife, native plants, wilderness and natural process of the mountain ecosystem in a land corridor from the Yukon down to Yellowstone.

Minerva Bloom

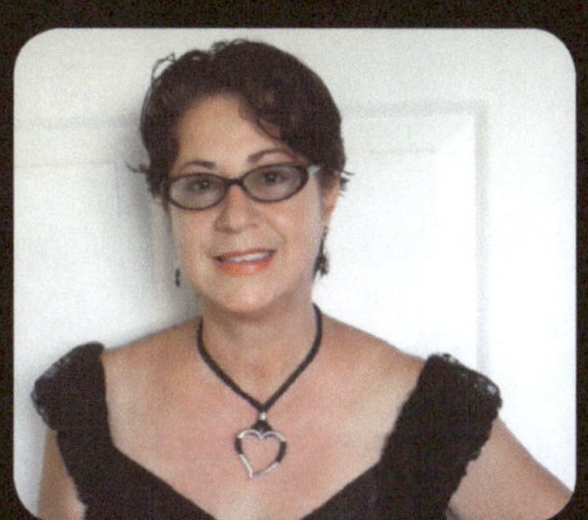

Minerva Bloom was born in a small mountain town in México. Minerva is a writer and photographer who has published several photography and poetry books. She currently resides in South Florida with her husband and 3 children.

Artist Statement: "*The concept of traveling light is hard for photographers. I try to keep it light because carrying heavy equipment for 8-12 hours a day is no fun. Nothing is easy about shouldering pounds of equipment for the ride. Also, new luggage regulations have forced photographers to be extra careful. I keep it simple and minimal and try to get by with one lens, or at times a little pocket camera. I carry a Canon DSLR, a lens cloth, a polarizer filter, flash, cable release, battery back-up, extra flash cards, a folded raincoat, a light tripod and pen and business cards. I also worry about weather-proofing, so my camera bag is weatherproofed. I have learned how to maximize more severe limitations than at home. A good pair of shoes is a must.*"

Markos Berndt

Markos Berndt is a landscape/nature photographer from Wisconsin. Despite the Wisconsin part, he doesn't like cheese nor does he drink alcohol, according to popular belief. He uses a tripod to keep his camera stable and it also serves as a weapon. He has been seen skipping along the shores of Lake Michigan with nothing on but his camera. Don't believe anything he says, he's as shady as they come.

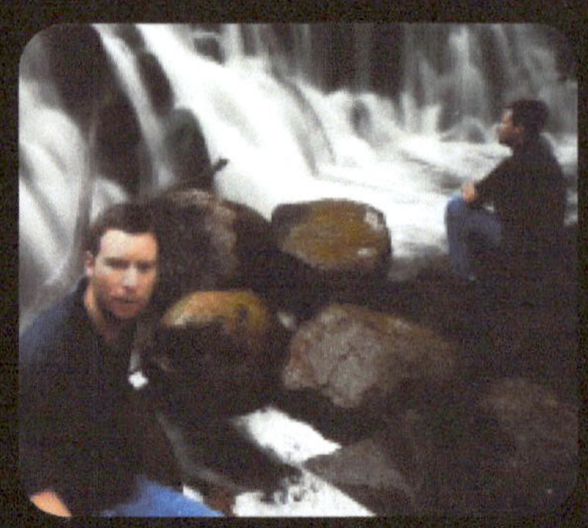

THE END

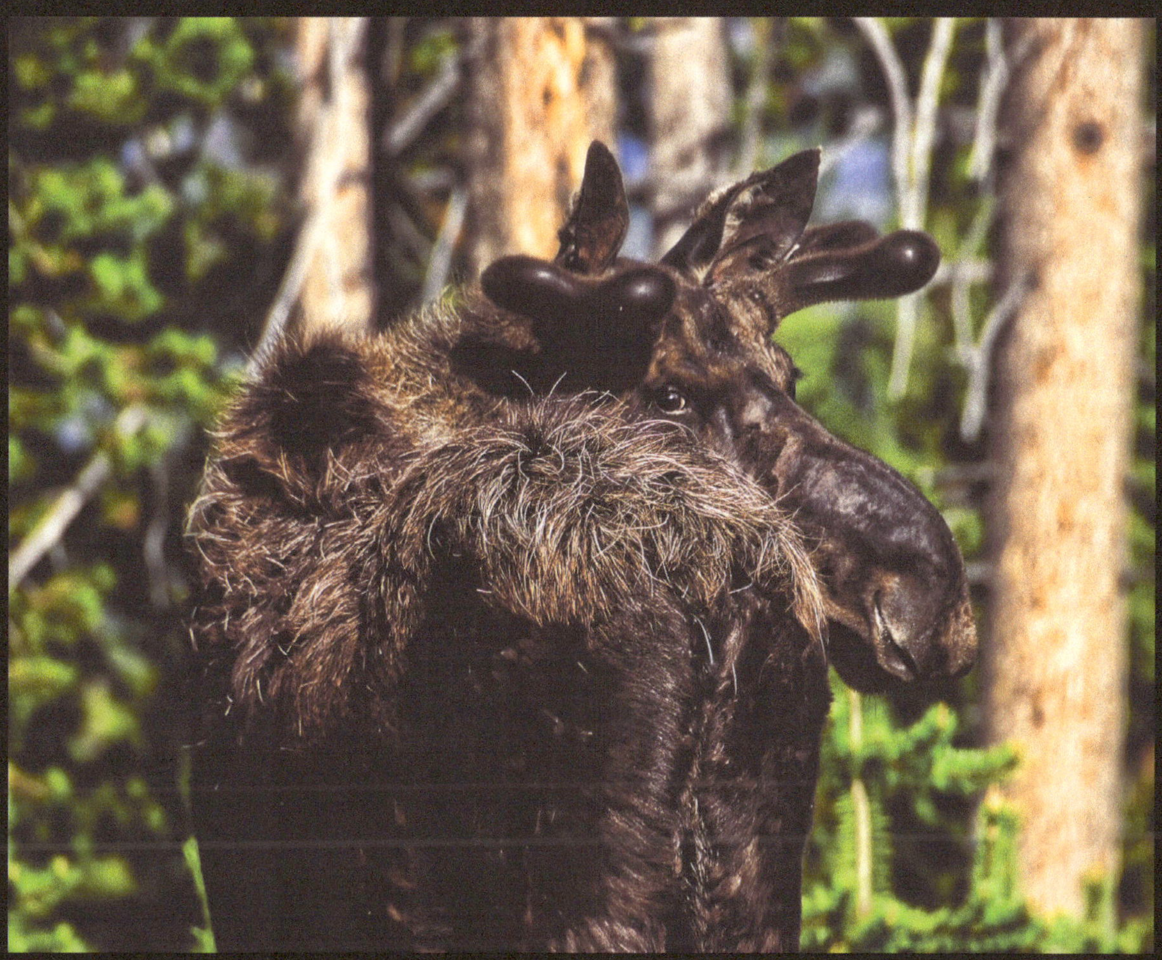

Image By Gary Glass

www.ingramcontent.com/pod-product-compliance
Lightning Source LLC
LaVergne TN
LVHW070140110826
845147LV00002B/292

* 9 7 8 0 5 5 7 9 2 2 7 0 3 *